DID I JUST HAVE A
SPIRITUAL AWAKENING,
OR WAS IT SOMETHING I ATE?

"Raw, authentic, bold, and insightful are just a few of the words that describe Jim Alstott's powerful book. If you are looking for pablum, theory, overused quotes, and motivational life coach drivel, you will have to look somewhere else. Jim's transformation journey was built with equal parts grace and sorrow, pain and gain, all incredibly woven together by his willingness to be vulnerable, drop a well-placed F-bomb in the most spiritual way possible, and have you come out feeling like you were walking side by side with him, as you find your better self in the process."

—John St. Augustine
Best-selling author of *Phenomena: Sacred Moments,*
*Messages, Memories & Other Sh*t I Can't Explain*

"Jim's words about his extraordinary awakening are bold, enlightening, and often hilarious. I wish more people could follow Jim's lead and share their experiences so honestly. If you've ever wondered about your place in this spiritual journey, do yourself a favor and grab this book."

—Jenniffer Weigel
Emmy Award–winning journalist and
author of *I'm Spiritual, Dammit!*

"*Did I Just Have a Spiritual Awakening, or Was It Something I Ate?* is an incredible, thought-provoking, and witty approach to having a spiritual awakening. Jim helps you question your journey, your experiences, and your connections, and find the truth by example and by learning to become comfortable being yourself. Jim's style of sharing is approachable, riveting, and filled with truth. I laughed, I cried, I had *aha!* moments. What more can you ask from a guide than that? I highly recommend and encourage you to dive into this book. You will be enlightened and changed, and you will start to question things for yourself."

—Gail Alexander
The No-Nonsense Intuitive and author of *Wakey-Wakey, It's Time!*
Humanity, Pay Attention and *Who You Really Are*

"This book is a must read for those of you who want to gigglegasm your way into enlightenment. The title of this book is so fitting, because by the time you finish it, you will truly understand that many times, the steps of the journey of discovering y/our magnificence on this planet can temporarily cause you to feel like you have an upset stomach. Jim will help you feel safe enough to understand that 'sensitive isn't a weakness—it's a spiritual superpower.' He will guide you to the confidence you need to realize that what others may call a 'weakness' of yours may, in fact, be your greatest connective superpower."

—Julie Foster, MD
Author of *Remembering Awake*

DID I JUST HAVE A SPIRITUAL AWAKENING, OR WAS IT SOMETHING I ATE?

JIM ALSTOTT

Pen & Publish
Saint Louis, Missouri

Copyright © 2026 Jim Alstott

All rights reserved. No part of this book may be reproduced or transmitted in any form or by any means, electronic or mechanical, including photocopying, recording, or by any information storage and retrieval system, without permission in writing from the publisher.

Published by Pen & Publish, LLC, USA

www.PenandPublish.com
info@PenandPublish.com

Saint Louis, Missouri
(314) 827-6567

Paperback ISBN: 978-1-956897-81-4
ebook ISBN: 978-1-956897-82-1
Library of Congress Control Number: 2026934870

Cover design and composition by Kerry Sue Müller
https://sidebar.design/

*For my family and friends, those who walk beside me
and those who watch over me from beyond the veil:
Thank you for your love and support, for the guidance
you've provided, the lessons you've taught me, and for
giving me a slap across the head when I need it. That
goes especially for my parents and grandparents.*

*Dutch, thank you for the laughs, love,
and the occasional pranks! BSC*

*To my boys, Jonathan, Nick, and Brady . . . my Big 4-0s:
I love you boys with all my heart and am so thankful you
chose me to be your dad. You have all brought me a lifetime of
love and happiness. I marvel at the young men you have each
become, and I look forward to seeing the great things you all
have in store in the years to come. I'm so proud of you all!*

*And to my wife, Becky:
Without you, none of this would have been possible.
Not the book, the podcast, and most of all, the boys.
LYM*

Contents

Foreword:
by Nate Scripture

Most of us can probably recall the scene in the court of the Royal Palace when Dorothy stood pleading with the Wizard of Oz to send her back home to Kansas after she and her trusty companions had made good on their promise to vanquish the Wicked Witch of the West. With the wizard's ominous voice echoing through the ether, giant flames erupting all around, plumes of smoke bellowing, and thunder booming in the background, Dorothy truly believed that the all-powerful wizard and his magic were real. As the wizard was in the process of reneging on his deal with Dorothy, and about to send her away, suddenly her trusty canine, Toto, got tangled up in a nearby piece of green curtain—pulling it back to expose someone feverishly tugging away on levers and switches like a master puppeteer. In that moment, with the curtain drawn wide open for all to see, the grand spectacle of smoke and mirrors came crashing down; a reality that seemed so real and tangible was now nothing more than an elaborate performance piece, a hoax, a manufactured stage disintegrating right before Dorothy's very own eyes. In a blink, the wizard was gone and instead remained an ordinary, old man. You could say Dorothy had peered behind not just a curtain, but through a type of veil, an illusory construct placed in her way like a type of control mechanism.

If you're asking yourself what the heck does Dorothy's revelation have to do with an "awakening," well the good news is that Jim will go on and spend the rest of this book explaining what happened when the curtain was yanked back for him, how he dealt with the aftermath, the enormous lessons learned, and then the series of experiences that ultimately led him to put pen to paper. Depending on your stage of awakening, this book will be many things to many people—a reminder, a coach, a companion, a how-to guide, an instructional manual, and more. Jim cleverly weaves together his love for music, dark humor, life stories, and spiritual encounters as the basis for the sections ahead. Maybe his greatest gift to all of you, though, is his vulnerability: sticking his neck out there so you can be equipped with real, tangible, maybe even, life-saving knowledge. So, if this book has made it into your hands, onto your tablet, or is currently dancing in your ears, consider it a blessing.

Jim and I have spoken extensively about our respective awakenings and the way in which they unfolded. We share many milestone moments, but in the end, ours were unique to us, as it will be (or has been) for you. Sometimes it can be hard to even identify if there is a single awakening moment that kicks off everything. For myself, it started gently over the course of a few months, and then it came on like a freight train. For others, it could be initiated by a near-death experience, the loss of a loved one, an ailment, a simple toe stub, or all manner of things. Some people will just "get it," while others like myself required more time to digest. No matter how you come to this realization, the important part of this whole awakening process is to hold firmly to faith, and while your life might feel like a construction site for the divine, it will be rebuilt in the way that is just right for your soul journey.

One of the miraculous treasures birthed out of Jim's experience was his creation of the *Drop the Needle Podcast,* where he explores almost everything plausible under the spiritual umbrella. If you know Jim, then you know he's like a forensic investigator constantly seeking clues, evidence, insights, and answers to fortify his case. Every episode he arrives with an open heart and mind, diligently pressing his guests to share meaningful information with his audience. He's listening, learning, and usually never dismisses anything outright. Through his podcast, he's been able to test others' insights against his own, which has strengthened his beliefs as well as corroborated many of his awakening experiences. He's compiled a lot of practical and useful information you can apply to your own life, and on his website, he has even gone so far to offer "quizzes" as a companion piece to this book—essentially questions to help you reflect about those blind spots, dark alleys, and the angles you might have missed. Jim will of course also dissect the stages and mechanics of what is actually happening during an awakening, so I won't expand too much here, but before we dive into the meat of his discoveries, it might be worth painting a basic picture of how one could view the greater purpose of an awakening through a slightly bizarre example.

Imagine playing a video game completely immersed and losing track of the fact that you've been sitting on a couch for hours on end as you unlock level after level like a crazed maniac. In this animated world, you can do anything you want: run over someone's legs in a Mercedes G-wagon, burn down a liquor store, or perform some sort of elaborate kung fu maneuver that propels your nemesis back through the gates of hell. You've unleashed all sorts of chaos in this universe without much of a care, but maybe this microcosm is rep-resentative of another reality and it's as real to the avatars in the game as your life is to you. Turning off the game console doesn't help because now we must consider: What if we've been trapped in a type of simulation? Is someone unleashing mayhem on us? Are we programmed players? Who built this elaborate ecosystem and why? How many layers does this go?

This is the moment we have to zoom out from our earthly reality and truly start to see things from a higher level of consciousness. It requires our ego to dissolve so we can begin to question the world we know, how we've been indoctrinated, the authoritative systems we are a part of, how we've been duped, played, and puppeted by our "leaders." Other perspectives also emerge. You'll begin to see people like souls on a quest rather than road-ragers on the beltway flipping you the bird. You'll start to understand the true value of peace and connection. You won't fall into the usual traps and your emotions won't get triggered so easily. You'll have gratitude for the smallest things in your life. You'll want to help people. And you'll see all of creation as a miracle as you walk through the world. Once you reach this stage of awareness, yes, you've officially cracked open. Congratulations! Not everyone makes it to this level, many will suffer or worse, and plenty of souls are simply not evolved or prepared to make such a leap. In short, all of this talk about awakening boils down to this: It's the moment when your awareness expands and aligns with higher consciousness. You become tapped into divinity in a meaningful, life-altering way. Curtains are ripped back and you're able to perceive your entire reality with fresh eyes, which continue to get sharper and sharper as you connect with your higher soul and God.

As Jim will remind you, the positive news is you're not alone even if the process itself feels lonely. There are others spread out all over the world going through these same exact personal shifts. You'll see these people at the checkout counter, on the back of a trash truck, at the local bank, and in your photography class. I doubt they exist in international call centers, but maybe. Awakened people are sprinkled all around and not always in the places you expect—some are in prison, some live in shelters, and some in psych wards. They might be hard to spot at first because they can be tucked away like Easter eggs. In fact, you are far less alone than you think. Waves and waves of souls are waking up all the time.

In the pages to come, Jim creates a type of guide for next level "Humaning." A GPS map, if you will, alerting you to the accidents, highway closures, and detours you might encounter further up the road. No matter what happens along your journey, walk with peace and love in your heart. Be grounded and aware of your own words and actions. Be present and be grateful. Be kind and compassionate, yet be strong and have even stronger boundaries. Stay humble. All the big positive shifts humanity wants to see in the world begins with you. Remember you carry the spark of God within—you hold the torch of the divine in your heart. You are not just a bag of flesh and bones wandering aimlessly on this earth. You have immense purpose, value, and many gifts to share with others. Last, but not least, awakenings are shaky, turbulent, and confronting. That's their nature by design—you're being shaken awake, asked to let go of your old programs, being placed onto a higher, more aligned timeline, and being reminded of your connection to God and all of creation. Do not freak out, do not spin out, and certainly do not check out. Send your roots deep into the earth so when the wind blows you keep steady. I'm pretty sure this guy Jim has some good ideas to help you along the way.

[End Scene. Close Curtain]

Nathaniel Scripture
Blue Tiger Healing Arts
www.bluetigerarts.com

Preface:
"Signs"

The Canadian band Five Man Electrical Band wrote their hit song "Signs" in 1971, and it seems quite fitting to start this literary party off with something that is all around us, but we're often blind to. I'm not talking about long-haired freaky people . . . necessarily, but I am talking about those little winks that are often so subtle, we don't see them unless the sign smacks us right in the face. Get used to this; you'll see a song kicking off nearly every section in this book.

But before we get too far ahead of ourselves, I need to set the stage for what you're about to experience. This isn't just a memoir, it's a roadmap for those moments when the universe decides to tap you on the shoulder and say, "Hey, pay attention, something bigger is happening here." That's precisely what happened to me on that ill-fated night on the beaches of Marco Island. Could it have been the theme park food I ate that day? Yeah, maybe. Could it have been from the pre-wedding, celebratory bender I was on the days leading up to that faithful night? Absolutely! It could have been that, too, but was it? Hell, I've heard of people having psychotic episodes after experiencing the loss of loved ones. It could have been any one of those things or pieces of all of them. But . . . was it? I don't have all of the answers to all of the questions, as you'll soon find out. However, what I do have are experiences, my experiences, and I'm betting that each one of you have had similar happenings in one form or another. So, why don't we sit back, relax, and see where this rocket ship takes us?

They say spirit, your guides, or departed loved ones often communicate through music. They also manipulate things with frequency or energy, lights, televisions, or that strange feeling when a song hits differently than usual. I love music; I studied music in school, majoring in vocal performance, and sang opera professionally for a short time. You'll see musical references throughout these pages because music has been the soundtrack to every major spiritual breakthrough in my life. It led me to launch my own podcast I host called *The Drop the Needle* podcast, which can be found on all your favorite podcast platforms. The connection between music and spiritual experience isn't coincidental; it's fundamental. You'll soon find that there are no coincidences in our lives, period. In each episode of the podcast, I ask the guest to help me create the soundtrack of their life. As I like to say, I believe everyone has a soundtrack to their life, if they just take a moment to think about it. Who knows, you might put together the Spiritual Soundtrack of your life while you're reading this book.

The musical thread that weaves through this entire journey began with a simple song that perfectly captures what I'm about to share with you. Paul McCartney wrote "Let 'Em In," a song about someone knocking at the door, asking to be let in. Sir Paul's message seems fitting for what I'm about to share with you, because sometimes the spiritual realm doesn't just knock politely—sometimes it kicks the door down and demands your attention.

The first time I realized that something beyond our physical world might exist, I was four years old, and let me tell you, that unique experience has stuck with me my entire life. It was my first core memory with the spiritual realm, and in many ways, it's the catalyst for my writing this book. More on that soon, but first a quick glimpse into where it all began ... When this bundle of joy—me—arrived in 1966, Plainfield, Illinois, the town I was raised in, had a population of approximately 2,100 people. My father, grandfather, and uncles built our house. The house was nothing special, really, but it weathered numerous storms, including a devastating tornado in 1991, and somehow survived one rambunctious only child, several dogs, and a couple of cats. My mom, Sharon, was an RN who worked in the emergency room for a nearby hospital. She was hardworking, kind, intelligent, and was quite a musician. Fun fact: Mom actually sang on one of Doc Severinsen's albums. (He was the *Tonight Show* band leader when Johnny Carson was the host.) She was a one-of-a-kind person. My dad, Jim, was as blue collar as they came. He worked for the gas company for nearly forty years, digging trenches, welding pipes, and jumping in and out of holes for his entire career. His work ethic was only matched by his temper at times. That house became ground zero for experiences I couldn't explain, experiences that would follow me throughout my life like a persistent melody you can't get out of your head.

This book, with its admittedly tongue-in-cheek title, *Did I Just Have a Spiritual Awakening, or Was it Something I Ate?*, chronicles those moments when something inexplicable intervened in my life. Moments that defied rational explanation but felt undeniably real. The title reflects the honest confusion that comes with spiritual awakening, and sometimes you genuinely don't know if what you're experiencing is profound divine intervention or just the result of that questionable gas station sushi you had for lunch.

I suspect you're reading this because you've had a similar experience or someone you know has shoved this book in your face and said, "Hey, you need to read this." Maybe a departed loved one visited in a dream that was just too vivid to ignore. Perhaps you've known things you couldn't possibly have known before they happened. Or maybe you've felt guided by something beyond yourself and your logical mind at critical moments in your life. If any of that resonates, then welcome to the club . . . the slightly confused, occasionally overwhelmed, but ultimately grateful club of people who've discovered that reality is far more expansive and mysterious than we were taught to believe. I'm no yogi or guru offering definitive answers about enlightenment or the afterlife. Consider me your slightly baffled fellow traveler—more like the Jungle Cruise captain at Disney World than a spiritual mentor—pointing out curious sights as we navigate these mysterious waters together. I'll do my best to be your guide through the weird, wonderful, and sometimes terrifying landscape of spiritual awakening.

I make every attempt to maintain a healthy dose of skepticism, which prevents me from spending every dime on 3 a.m. infomercial products or handing over my credit card to "Ms. Martha, the Mystical Psychic," who charges thirty dollars for the first three minutes, by the way. Not that I have firsthand knowledge of that, mind you. There have been times when I felt more lost than others, times when I questioned my own sanity, and times when I wanted to close that spiritual door and go back to believing that what you see is all there is. But here's the thing: I'll admit something I can't explain has been happening with me and around me for as long as I can remember. Some psychic mediums are genuinely gifted and seem like angels on Earth, people who've dedicated their lives to helping others connect with something greater than themselves. Then there's the other side, the grimy bottom dwellers who are ready to take every dime from you in a weakened emotional state, without hesitation or remorse. You can typically smell them coming, and if you have any intuition, you'll feel them too. Learning to distinguish between genuine spiritual guidance and spiritual charlatans is part of the journey, and I'll share what I've learned along the way about navigating these sometimes-murky waters.

This book contains profanity, which I've been told may turn some readers off. If you're offended by profanity, I apologize. This is just who I am authentically, foul-mouthed at times, but eloquent, kind, and articulate at others. I believe it's a reflection of who we are as a collective, and you will get to experience the good, the bad, the ugly, and the divine in my life.

The spiritual journey isn't always pretty, and it doesn't always come wrapped in gentle, euphemistic language. Sometimes the most profound truths come through raw, honest expression, including the occasional F-bomb when the situation warrants it. We're all adults here, so I hope we can be comfortable talking and swearing as we skip along my life's timeline. This authentic approach to spirituality means you'll get the whole truth—the moments of divine connection alongside the moments of doubt, confusion, and yes, occasional colorful language—because that's how real spiritual awakening happens: messy, unpredictable, and completely authentic. I'm inviting you on a journey that's likely familiar to many of you, times when something inexplicably steps in to save our ass or save the asses of those around us.

Are you ready? Let's go.

Spiritual Summary

When Spirit comes a-knockin', it doesn't always knock politely. Sometimes it kicks the damn door down, grabs you by the collar, and demands your attention. You don't need to be a guru or have all the answers to recognize when something bigger is happening; you just need to pay attention and stay open while keeping your bullshit detector intact. This journey can be a little messy, confusing, and occasionally terrifying, but if you've ever had an experience you couldn't explain away with logic, congratulations, you're already in the club. Consider this book your permission slip to explore the weird, the wonderful, and the "what the hell was that?" moments that have been following you around your entire life.

Here's a public service announcement for everyone.

Throughout the book, I'll be sharing experiences that happened to me during the various stages of my spiritual journey. At the end of each section, I will provide you with a spiritual summary, or section wrap-up. The journey we're about to embark on together isn't just my story—it's a mirror that might help you see your own spiritual awakening more clearly, whether you're just beginning or you're years into the process and looking for validation that you're not completely losing your mind. Trust me, that validation is important. When you're experiencing things that defy logical explanation, knowing that others have walked this path before you can be the difference between embracing your awakening and running from it in fear.

At the end of the book, you'll find a QR code to my website, where you'll find the spiritual summaries along with questions that will hopefully spark a memory, or something for you to revisit an experience you've had, which may help you in wrapping your mind around this whole spiritual awakening/journey we're on together. I hope you find this as helpful and enlightening as it was for me to write the book. These questions aren't meant to be homework assignments— they're invitations to deeper self-reflection and opportunities to recognize your own spiritual patterns and experiences. I only wish there was something like that when I started this bumpy road of awakening.

Also, this might be the perfect time for you to create your Spiritual Soundtrack. Give it a try; you might be surprised by what music comes to you. Oh, yes, and have fun with it! Music is an incredible way to raise your vibration and open you up to even bigger things.

Speaking of Spiritual Soundtrack . . . You'll notice nifty QR codes throughout the book. If you take your phone out and scan the QR code, you'll be able to listen to my playlist while reading. You gotta love technology, right? Anyway, those are my suggestions for you, and my way of saying thank you for purchasing my book. So, thank you again!

"Everything Is Beautiful":
The Unique Path of Spiritual Awakening

The transition from my childhood experiences with the spiritual realm to understanding there might be a pattern to this madness came much later in life. It wasn't until I began researching spiritual awakening that I realized my experiences weren't just a series of random, weird occurrences; they were part of a recognizable journey that countless others have traveled. Like pieces of a puzzle I didn't know I was assembling, everything started to make sense when I discovered there was actually a framework for what I'd been experiencing all along.

In March of 1970, Ray Stevens released a single titled "Everything Is Beautiful." The lyrics remind everyone that everything and everyone is beautiful in their own way, and that we should not close our minds to things, and that beauty lies in the eye of the beholder. This song became the perfect anthem for what I discovered about spiritual awakening—there's no one-size-fits-all approach to connecting with the divine. So the path (or steps) to my, yours, or our spiritual awakening is unique and special to each of us. In my research on identifying what exactly a spiritual awakening is, I was a little perplexed by what I found. I initially thought that there had to be some magical, mystical formula that applied to everyone. I quickly found that one size does *not* fit all in the spiritual fitting room. So in my case, I wasn't on a mountain top in Nepal, sipping tea with enlightened monks. As I mentioned earlier, I was on the beautiful sandy beaches of Marco Island: no llamas, no sherpas, just me, barefoot in the sand, and the occasional nasty-ass sand flea.

The realization of this was both liberating and frustrating. Part of me wanted a clear roadmap, a step-by-step guide that would tell me exactly what to expect and when to expect it. But the deeper truth is that spiritual awakening is as individual as a fingerprint—no two journeys look precisely the same; even though they may share common elements, the journey is yours alone. Well, not exactly alone, I'm here too, but you get what I mean, right? Your path is just that, it's *your* path. It's not mine, your sister's, your brother's. It's especially not your dear Aunt Edna's journey—God only knows where you'd end up!

So, what exactly is an "awakening" anyway? Some people might see it as a sharp break from reality, an epic crumbling of the programming you've been conditioned under. It's that moment where you can see your life and the world from a completely different perspective. Hindu mystics refer to the word *māyā*, which means illusion, in spiritual terms. In some ways it's just what has been hidden from you in plain sight. From a spiritual and metaphysical perspective, an "awakening" is "leveling up" to a higher plane of consciousness where you gain access to deeper wisdom and truth about the world and beyond. Many movies have attempted to portray this peeling back of reality. Here's an example that comes to mind. It would be similar to the experience Neo had in the movie *The Matrix* upon discovering he was living in a structured simulation, an illusionary world created much like a video game. His choice was to take the red pill or the blue pill. The blue pill would take him back to blissful ignorance, the comfortable world he knew so well. The red pill would teach him about the unsettling truth and the false world he was born into.

Let's just say I got "red-pilled" in a huge way without choice, and now there's absolutely no going back. Once you peer behind the metaphorical curtain, much like Dorothy in *The Wizard of Oz,* you can never unsee what had been hidden in front of you all this time. The movie *The Truman Show* also perfectly demonstrates that awakening moment when the world you thought you knew so well was all one big illusion. Truman eventually learns that he was living in a highly manipulated simulation with heavy programming by society, his friends, and even his loved ones. Once he figured out he was trapped inside of a reality show, he was able to break free and exit the matrix—much like ascending to a higher level of consciousness. So that's what we are talking about, folks. Ascension is your consciousness rising to new levels, and the first stage is really what we are calling the "awakening" phase. Perhaps the one person who can shed the most light on this subject is one of my favorite authors and teachers, Dolores Cannon.

Dolores Cannon was an American author, hypnotherapist, and is considered by many to be the leader of the New Age movement. Ms. Cannon was also a pioneer in past-life regressions via the use of hypnotherapy. Through her decades of work with thousands of clients, she began to notice patterns in the spiritual awakening process that transcended individual differences.

Ms. Cannon outlined a twelve-step process for experiencing a spiritual awakening, which became a framework that helped countless people understand where they were in their spiritual journey and what might be next.

The steps are as follows:

1. The Awakening
2. Seeking
3. Questioning
4. Self-Discovery
5. Healing
6. Integration
7. Service to Others
8. Expanded Consciousness
9. Intuition and Guidance
10. Manifestation
11. Unity Consciousness
12. Mastery and Service

Others have outlined the stages of a spiritual awakening in five steps, seven, ten, and as many as nineteen steps. I don't think the number of steps is significant; as I mentioned previously, we all go through different things at different times, and in different ways. What is important is that everyone starts, and what I'm finding is, your journey may never end. My experience certainly took a few wild turns along the way, but I started where most everyone else begins, and that's the awakening. The beauty of Ms. Cannon's framework isn't in its rigid structure—it's in its recognition that spiritual growth follows certain universal patterns while allowing for infinite individual variation. Some people may experience multiple stages simultaneously, while others may revisit earlier stages for deeper healing. Others may skip around in what appears to be a random order but is actually perfectly orchestrated by their soul's divine needs.

The awakening stage is often marked by a pivotal point in your life when something significant occurs, prompting you to contemplate life's deeper meaning. At this stage, many people encounter experiences that lead to new insights, beliefs, or ways of thinking. You may have a strong desire to start taking yoga, explore practices like reiki, or delve into spiritual pursuits and literature. You might even begin to, God forbid, meditate and connect with your higher self, or even God. Woo to the woo. Or if you happen to be me, you dive into every freaking one of those things I just mentioned with the enthusiasm of a kid in a candy store. Keep in mind, there is no wrong or right in what you decide to take an interest in; whatever you're called to do is absolutely correct. The spiritual awakening process has its own intelligence, and it will guide you toward exactly what you need, when you need it.

One thing is for sure, and let me tell you, there's no mistaking it, you will quickly know you're experiencing, let's call it a "spiritual rite of passage." You might brush it off at first, even thinking you're having a psychotic episode, but I assure you that's far from the truth. It's also important to note, not everyone incarnated on Earth will go through this process—some souls are simply not ready to evolve at this time. This is why there is much chaos across many parts of the planet—there are still plenty of young souls participating in lower states of consciousness. The conditioning and programming is so heavy in the world that most souls are far too caught up in false narratives and old beliefs to see through the illusion. The silver lining is that each awakened soul can ignite the light within another, and before long, there's a domino effect gaining unstoppable momentum and shifting the consciousness of the whole Earth to new unknown levels. It's almost like the old commercial: "You tell two friends, and you tell two friends, and so on, and so on." It's also important we honor everyone's soul journey regardless of if they're "awake" or not. Our focus is to heal ourselves so we become part of the solution, not add to the existing problems.

I'd like to address the glowing, translucent elephant in the room now, if I may. There is nothing wrong with you if you have a desire to dive down any or all of the esoteric rabbit holes above. You're not weird, you aren't sick, and you sure as hell don't deserve to be banished to the Isle of Misfit Toys. You are absolutely fine; you are better than fine. You are perfect where you are and just as you are. And you are always welcome in our slightly irregular circle, anytime you'd like. This acceptance and normalization of spiritual curiosity is crucial because so many people feel isolated or ashamed when they begin having these experiences or interests. Society has conditioned us to view spiritual exploration with suspicion or to relegate it to the "fringe" category, but the truth is that spiritual seeking is one of the most natural and human things we can do.

Spiritual Summary

There's no magical, mystical formula for waking up spiritually. Your journey is as unique as a fingerprint, and it sure as hell doesn't require llamas, sherpas, or a mountaintop in Nepal. Once you've been red-pilled and peeked behind the curtain, there's no going back to blissful ignorance, so you might as well buckle up and enjoy the ride. And if you're feeling like a misfit because you're suddenly interested in meditation, energy healing, or any of this woo-woo stuff, just relax, there's nothing wrong with you; you're not broken, you're waking up. You don't belong on the Island of Misfit Toys; you belong right here, in this slightly irregular circle of awakening souls who are figuring it out as they go.

"Oh, What a Night":
My First Experience Seeing Dead People

The transition from explaining the framework of spiritual awakening to sharing my actual experiences brings us to where it all began—with a four-year-old boy, a deceased great-grandfather, and a moment that would define the next fifty-five years of my life. This is where theory meets reality, where the abstract concept of spiritual awakening becomes as real as the breath in your lungs.

"Oh, What a Night"
Frankie Valli

Frankie Valli sang about a special night in late December back in '63, and what a special time it was for him. My special night was April 10, 1970. While Frankie's song was about falling in love, my experience was about discovering that love doesn't end when someone leaves their physical body—it just takes on new forms and finds new ways to express itself. You might wonder how I could remember something that occurred when I was four years old. Well, the answer is quite simple: If you saw a glowing version of your great-grandfather, I'm confident it would stick with you, too. I also believe I'm supposed to remember it so I can share it with you. Some experiences are so significant, so life-altering, that they burn themselves into our consciousness with permanent clarity.

April 10, 1970, marked the day my great-grandfather, Delbert Harold Rinehart, passed away. I vaguely remember he'd gone into the hospital with an illness related to a bladder or kidney problem—details weren't discussed around my young ears at that time. In those days, medical information was kept from children, as if not knowing would somehow protect us from the reality of mortality. At four years old, bedtime was around eight-thirty, and that particular night followed the same routine as always—bath, pajamas, story, prayers, lights out. Nothing in the evening ritual suggested that the world was about to shift on its axis and introduce me to a reality I wouldn't fully understand for decades. As I slept that April night, something woke me. I was drawn by an inexplicable certainty, like in movies when a person stares blankly and appears to be pulled by an invisible force, beckoning, calling them near. This wasn't the gradual awakening you experience from natural sleep cycles—this was sudden, purposeful, as if someone had gently but persistently called my name until I opened my eyes. I somehow knew I needed to check my closet—not because I thought there was a monster, but because someone, or something, was calling for me and was waiting. The knowing was absolute, the way a child knows when their mother is in the next room or when something important is about to happen. There was no fear in this knowing, only a sense of being needed, of having an appointment I had to keep.

A soft glow leaked from beneath the sliding wooden door. Not the harsh white and red from my Bozo the Clown nightlight, but something gentler, warmer, more welcoming. This light had a quality I'd never seen before—it seemed to emanate peace itself, creating a bubble of calm in what should have been an ordinary, slightly scary childhood moment. I crept from bed, in my zip-up onesie pajamas with the oh-so-comfortable vinyl footies, trying to be as quiet as possible, and eased the door back slowly. The anticipation was electric, but not frightening—more like Christmas-morning anticipation, mixed with the solemnity of something sacred about to unfold. There sat my great-grandfather, Delbert, on my clothes hamper, looking exactly as he always had but somehow more vibrant, more present than he'd ever been in life. He acknowledged me with the four-fingered wave adults reserve for children—palm still, fingers dancing—then opened his mouth and began tapping his lips, creating the familiar popping sound that always brought a smile to my face. The special greeting that was uniquely ours, and one I clearly remember to this day. It was our secret language of love, a ritual that belonged only to us, and here he was, honoring it one last time. I wasn't afraid. How could I be? This was my great-grandpa doing precisely what he always did—popping his lips and making me smile. The fact that he had a slight glow around the edges seemed perfectly logical to my four-year-old self. Children haven't yet learned what's "impossible," so they accept magic as naturally as they accept breakfast cereal and bedtime stories.

So, it was reasonable that after our brief encounter, I ran downstairs to share the news with my mom. In my child's mind, this was wonderful news that needed to be shared immediately—Great-Grandpa had come to visit, just like he always did, and she would want to know about it. My mom's response: "Shh . . . don't say that! You just heard us talking." But I hadn't heard anyone talking. How could I? I was asleep, then awakened by someone or something telling me to walk over to my closet, open the door, and say hello. I get it—I wouldn't have been too eager to take on that conversation as a parent either. How do you explain to a four-year-old that what they just experienced challenges everything adults have been taught about the nature of reality? How do you validate a child's spiritual experience when you're not sure you believe in such things yourself? My mom must have picked up on the fact my feelings were a little hurt when she dismissed my story as being nonsense, and marched alongside me up the stairs. She, of course, tucked me in and gave me the famous four kisses on my forehead. Whenever my mom said goodnight or goodbye, I would always get those four kisses on my forehead in the sign of the cross. It didn't matter to her if I was four years old or twenty-four years old, it was always the same thing. So, with a quick spin and a glance over the shoulder, I got my goodnight, and the door closed. It was the last time we ever spoke about Great-Grandpa in the closet. I can say that I would frequently go back to my closet and peek in to see if my great-grandpa was dropping by to say hello again. Unfortunately, that was the only time he dropped in for a visit.

Later, I learned my great-grandfather had died hours before I saw him in my closet. His unique gesture remains etched in my mind to this day, and even at fifty-nine years old, it still brings a smile to my face when I think of it. The timing wasn't coincidental—it was intentional, a loving good-bye orchestrated from the other side. I now understand why my mom reacted as she did. I honestly couldn't tell you if my immediate reaction wouldn't have been the same in her position. I'm open to these things, but who wouldn't be a little taken aback or skeptical hearing this from their four-year-old son? The challenge for parents in these situations is enormous—how do you respond to something that defies your understanding while still honoring your child's experience?

There you have it—my very first experience with deceased loved ones, mediumship, spirituality, or "wackadoo-ness," as some may lovingly call it. This moment became the foundation for everything that would follow, the first note in a spiritual symphony that would play throughout my entire life. This experience established several important patterns that would repeat again and again in my life: the certainty of the knowing, the naturalness of the supernatural, the immediate impulse to share the experience with others, and the challenge of having these experiences validated by people who haven't had them themselves. These patterns would become familiar companions on my path, showing up again and again as the universe continued to reveal its mysteries to me.

Spiritual Summary

My spiritual journey didn't begin on a mountaintop or during a meditation retreat. My journey started in a closet with a four-year-old in vinyl-footie pajamas and a departed great-grandfather doing our special lip-popping greeting one last time. Kids haven't yet learned what's "impossible," so they accept visits from the other side as naturally as breakfast cereal, which might be why Spirit chose that moment to introduce itself. Love doesn't end when someone leaves their body; it just finds new ways to show up. Sometimes glowing gently on a clothes hamper in the middle of the night. That moment etched itself into my consciousness and set the stage for every spiritual experience that would follow over the next fifty-five years.

"Only the Beginning":
Embracing Sensitivity as a Spiritual Gift

The aftermath of that first spiritual encounter with my great-grandfather set the stage for how I would navigate similar experiences throughout my childhood and beyond. Looking back, I can see that this moment wasn't just a one-time visitation—it was an initiation into a way of being that would define much of my life. The door that opened that night would never fully close, and through it would come experiences that would both challenge and validate everything I thought I knew about reality.

"Beginnings"
Chicago

Chicago's "Beginnings" captures the feeling perfectly—it was only the beginning, and it was a feeling I want to feel forever. That encounter with Great-Grandpa Delbert wasn't an ending—it was the opening note of a lifelong spiritual symphony that would continue to play, sometimes softly in the background, and sometimes demanding center stage.

Humor has always been my coping mechanism for the unexplainable and stressful times in my life. Growing up, I loved comedy films and albums, finding comfort in laughter when confronted with life's heavier shit. This tendency to deflect with humor also became my default response to spiritual experiences. If I could joke about it, I wouldn't have to fully deal with what was happening or, more importantly, face the potential ridicule that came with taking these experiences too seriously. For some reason, I preferred laughter over heavier emotions. I still do. Humor became my spiritual armor, protecting me from both my own fears about what these experiences meant and from others' potential judgment of my "overactive imagination." Ever since I can remember, I've been called a sensitive person. Can you relate? Depending on who you're talking to, this can be a great thing or not-so-great thing, followed by a list of names: wuss, wimp, pussy, and one of my personal favorites, fag. The last one is no longer acceptable to use, but it was a name someone, I'm sure, threw at me several times in my life. Quite honestly, it was never an appropriate term to use. Especially since I was involved in the arts at an early age, participating in nonmainstream activities typically brings out the societal label maker. Just to be completely accurate, I was labeled a "band fag" by those nonmusical members of my community. By the way, I was called something different late in life that provided me with a little more insight, and that was an "empath." What's an empath, you ask? Well, an empath is someone who is super sensitive to the feelings of others and takes them on as their own. Now, this goes way beyond someone sympathizing with another person. Empaths literally feel other people's emotions, which can be seen as both a gift at times, and freaking brutal in others. Allow me to put it another way. Imagine an empath as being an emotional tuning fork. When you strike a tuning fork and bring it near another tuning fork, the unstruck fork begins to vibrate, which is known as sympathetic vibration.

So when you're an empath/emotional tuning fork, you pick up on other emotional frequencies around you and it begins to resonate with you too. Please keep in mind, this isn't only when someone is angry or sad, it also happens when a person is happy. Something else to consider with an empath is that picking up these emotional frequencies is not a choice. This sensitivity I'm referring to is an innate part of their nervous system, which often leads to several core experiences:

Emotional absorption: When they soak up emotions from others, making it difficult to differentiate where their feelings end and another's begins.

Reading the room: Empaths have an innate ability to pick up on the "vibe" of the space they're in. They can walk into a room and immediately sense any underlying tensions or happiness, even if no one is outwardly expressing those emotions.

Exhaustion: By having the emotional vacuum on all the time, it can be absolutely draining and overwhelming for an empath. This is especially true in large crowds. Empaths often need a quiet place, where they can decompress and recharge.

Intuition: Because empaths are so attuned to the subtlest cues, they often have incredibly strong instincts about people and situations. They can easily tell when someone is being dishonest, because their energy doesn't match the words that are being spoken. Right now, you might be saying to yourself, what's the big deal, everyone has empathy, right? Well, hold on a minute, there is a difference between having empathy and being an empath. Most people have empathy, which is the ability to understand and feel concern for what another person may be going through or experiencing. Here's where it's different though: An empath's experience is far more intense. Instead of simply nodding their head in an understanding way as a friend tells them their sad story, an empath will begin to actually feel that same sadness themselves. This ability to literally feel the sadness of the other individual is what sets them apart.

Remember, I was born in 1966. The word *empath* hardly even existed back then. We also didn't have the social acceptability filters we have now. I wish we had—that would have saved me from some emotional scars and a few physical ones, too. Not to mention the countless hours and dollars spent on therapy. The world was a different place then, where sensitivity was seen as weakness, especially in boys, and spiritual experiences were often dismissed as attention-seeking behavior or mental instability. But here's what I've learned through decades of experience and spiritual growth: Being labeled "sensitive" wasn't an insult—it was an accurate description of a spiritual gift that most people are too afraid or too numb to embrace. The sensitivity that made me a target for childhood bullies was the same sensitivity that allowed me to perceive spiritual communication, to feel energy shifts in rooms, and to sense things about people that others couldn't detect.

Let me share some information about children and their openness to spiritual events. Understanding the science and psychology behind childhood spiritual experiences helps validate what many of us experienced but were taught to dismiss or hide. My childhood encounter with my great-grandfather isn't unusual. Children everywhere report similar experiences—seeing departed loved ones, sensing presences, or knowing things they couldn't possibly know. Science offers several explanations that, rather than dismissing these experiences, actually help us understand why they might be more common and more valid than adults typically acknowledge. At four years old, my brain was only beginning to develop the filters that would later help me categorize experiences as "possible" or "impossible." Neurologists suggest this developmental openness might explain why children seem more receptive to spiritual encounters. The adult brain, with all its conditioning and societal programming, has learned to filter out information that doesn't fit into accepted reality, but the child's brain hasn't yet learned or installed those limitations.

Developmental psychologists believe children haven't internalized cultural norms against discussing such experiences. They haven't yet learned that certain topics are "weird" or "unacceptable," so they report their experiences with the same matter-of-fact honesty they bring to everything else in their world. Whatever the explanation, I now understand why it freaked my mom out so much and why she reacted the way she did. The clash between a child's natural spiritual openness and an adult's conditioned skepticism creates tension that many families struggle to navigate. What freaks us out as adults often seems perfectly normal to children. While she heard what she thought was a child's imagination running wild, contradicting her understanding of reality, I simply saw my great-grandfather doing what he always did—making me smile. The difference in our perspectives wasn't about right or wrong—it was about learned limitations versus unlimited possibilities.

Have you ever walked in on a child playing alone, carrying on a conversation with someone who appears to be sitting across from them? I'm referring to pauses where questions are asked and thoughtful answers are provided. Some conversations are clearly with Mr. Bunny, a favorite stuffed animal, positioned in a chair. As for the other well-thought-out conversations with someone you can't physically see, well, I'll leave that up to you to decide. These moments of childhood interaction with invisible presences are far more common than most adults realize or acknowledge. The question isn't whether these interactions are happening—any parent who's observed closely has witnessed them—the question is what we do with that information and how we choose to interpret and respond to these experiences. I simply ask that we proceed with an open mind and an open heart, and see where this takes us. And that's coming from one wuss to another, assuming you were called that too. If you've made it this far in the book, there's a good chance you understand what it's like to be labeled as "too sensitive," and maybe it's time we reclaimed that sensitivity as the gift it actually is.

The journey from that first spiritual encounter to understanding its significance would take decades, but every step along the way reinforced the same truth: Sensitivity isn't a flaw to be corrected—it's a spiritual antenna that allows us to receive information and experiences that can guide, comfort, and heal us throughout our lives. What they called weakness was actually my greatest strength, though it would take me years to understand that fully.

Spiritual Summary

Being called "sensitive" isn't a weakness—it's a spiritual superpower that most people are too afraid or too numb to embrace. Children see spirits and have spiritual experiences because they haven't been taught yet that it's "impossible." The filters we develop as adults aren't always protecting us; in fact, they're oftentimes blocking us from experiencing the magic that's always been there, which has been there since the day we were born. Your sensitivity, your ability to feel and/or sense what others can't—that's not something to apologize for or hide behind with humor, like me. That's your direct line to the divine. Trust yourself and try it on for size.

"It's a Small World After All": When Crisis Becomes Spiritual Awakening

The transition from childhood spiritual encounters to adult spiritual awakening rarely follows a straight line. For me, that path wound through decades of burying my sensitivity under layers of weight, denial, and desperate attempts to fit into a world that seemed to have no room for people like me. Between that four-year-old boy seeing his great-grandfather and the man I would become, there were years of trying to shut down the very gifts that would eventually save my life.

"It's a Small World"
The Sherman Brothers

Disney's classic song and theme park ride about our interconnected world kept playing in my head. "It's a small, small world . . ." Little did I know how prophetic that would prove to be, not just in terms of unexpected connections, but in understanding that the spiritual realm is always closer than we think, especially when we need it most. The irony wasn't lost on me that some of my most profound spiritual insights would come during a family vacation to what many call the "happiest place on Earth." Sometimes the universe chooses the most unlikely settings for our greatest breakthroughs, perhaps because we're caught off guard and our usual defenses are down.

My family and I visited both Disney theme parks, ate a lot of food, and spent a shit ton of money. Throughout our day, I faked my enthusiasm, put on a smile while constantly wiping away rivers of sweat from my face, and was almost entirely zoned out and disconnected from everything. The disconnect was profound—here I was, surrounded by joy and magic, and I felt like I was watching it all through thick glass, unable to touch or be touched by any of it. My feet were swollen, the sun was cooking me like an overdone chicken tender under a heat lamp, my head was aching to holy hell, and the lines, oh my *God*, the fucking lines that seemed to go on for miles, with the screaming toddlers, began to send me into a spin. I could no longer ignore the thoughts running wild in my head—they were getting louder and louder like Space Mountain barreling down on me. Two of my final conversations with my dad stayed on a perpetual loop over the two days at the happiest places on Earth. The first was "It looks like you have the weight of the world on your shoulders," and the second was "Life's too short to be unhappy all the time." These weren't just casual observations—they were profound statements from a man who rarely expressed emotional awareness, and they hit me like a freight train. The reason the weight of the world comment was repeating had a lot to do with the fact that I was really heavy, a.k.a. fat. How heavy? I didn't know and was afraid of stepping on a scale. Most of the scales I had stepped on, most importantly, the digital scale in my home, read "Error" when I stepped on it. My scale at home only went up to three hundred and fifty pounds. So I know I weighed more than three hundred and fifty pounds, but how much more? I had no clue. And why in God's name would anyone want to step on a scale and have it read "Error," unless they wanted to be made fun of by anyone in the vicinity, or if they wanted to bet someone they could break a freaking scale every time they stepped on it? The humiliation of breaking a scale became a metaphor for how broken I felt inside—too much for the tools designed to measure normal human existence.

I was in full-on crisis mode in terms of my physical health at this point. In a way, I was a "walking and talking" NDE (Near-Death Experience) each day that I woke up. If you don't know, NDEs are essentially when someone gets way too close to checking out permanently—like during a surgery gone wrong or a horrific car accident—and they get a cosmic "coming attractions" of what's next. We're talking the full spiritual IMAX-on-steroids experience: floating outside your body while looking down at yourself, zooming through a tunnel toward a bright light, getting your entire life played back like a Netflix binge you can't stop, and sometimes having a reunion with Grandpa or other beings who tell you it's not your time yet. The whole thing happens outside normal space and time, which explains how someone can feel like Gilligan and the Skipper took them on a three-hour tour of the afterlife in the thirty seconds their heart stopped. Most people come back from these experiences completely transformed—suddenly death isn't scary, life is precious, and they're way more spiritual than the dude saying "namaste" while trying to hug you at your local yoga studio (remind me to tell you guys about that one later). Sure, some folks have scary NDEs that need some therapy to unpack, but either way, it's like getting a software upgrade for your soul. Bottom line: NDEs are the universe's spoiler alert, showing someone the ending of the movie before sending them back to finish watching their life with a newfound point of view.

So yeah, I was hefty enough for an NDE, maybe worse. Every morning became a small miracle, not in a grateful way, but in a terrifying way—would my body be able to carry me through another day?

The other phrase . . . "Life's too short to be unhappy all the time." I had never experienced an extended period of unhappiness in my life before, but I was now in the thick of it, and it had been this way for quite a while. Here I am, on a vacation with my family, realizing it's about making memories, not rehashing them, but I couldn't snap out of this fog. All I know is that I needed help, and unfortunately, I really didn't have anyone I could talk to about what was going on. For whatever reason, I knew I would find an answer; I didn't know where it would come from, but I was hoping for the answer to come sooner rather than later. This knowing—that help was coming—was itself a spiritual experience, though I wouldn't recognize it as such for years. Sometimes our soul communicates with us through inexplicable certainty about things we have no logical reason to believe.

Nearly all spiritual awakenings begin with a feeling that something needs to change, whether it's a personal crisis or a longing for something more meaningful in life. At this moment in time, I checked both of those boxes for sure. This wasn't just depression or a rough patch—this was what spiritual teachers call "divine dissatisfaction," a soul-level restlessness that can't be fixed with external changes or positive thinking. It's the discomfort that comes when your soul knows it's time to grow but your ego is desperately trying to maintain the status quo. Unfortunately for me, my discomfort was about to increase tenfold and my ego was about to get sucker punched in the face. We wrapped up our final day at the park. Thank goodness it was over. I only had to buy two shirts that day. I sweated through the first two, and was on to number three of the day. Central Florida is warm, especially when you're extra, extra husky. For all of you who are unfamiliar with the Husky section of the boys' clothing department, go ahead and get a chuckle and GTS. (GTS is what I lovingly refer to as "Google That Shit." Google is fucking amazing; we can search for so many things in a millisecond … It's nuts.) That's the section I used to have to go to as a kid to get my clothes. I guess some marketing expert decided Husky was kinder than Schlubby-Sized. The humor here was my way of deflecting from the pain, but the pain was real and profound—the humiliation of not fitting into regular-sized clothes, of sweating through multiple shirts in a day, of being physically unable to keep up with my own family. Each of these experiences was chipping away at my soul, preparing me for the spiritual intervention that was about to come. I want you to imagine this for a moment. You've been walking around Walt Disney World all day; it was in the mid-to-upper 80s, full-on swamp humidity, and you weigh an unknown amount at this time, but it's certainly over three hundred and fifty pounds. It is 8:45 p.m., and you're finally returning to your hotel room. What would you want to do? Go on, guess. "Hey, can we go see the new *Star Wars* movie?" my youngest says.

I didn't even have a chance to fully acknowledge the question when my wife said, "Sure, let's walk to the theater; it's not that far away."

My chin hit my chest so fast that I hurt my neck a little. "Can I at least take a shower?"

"Yes, but make it quick."

The universe has a sense of humor about timing. Just when you think you can't take another step, life kicks you in the ass and has you take a few thousand more. But sometimes those extra steps are exactly what you need to reach the place where transformation becomes possible. I'm going to fast forward for the sake of all involved and get to the part when we had just left the movie theater after seeing *Star Wars: Episode IX—The Rise of Skywalker*. As we began walking back to our hotel, thoughts started rolling in again, and I was slowing my pace even more than usual. I urged my family to go ahead of me and told them I would meet them back in the room in a while. "I'm just going to take my time and enjoy the warm night and the stars." Another moment of truth here: I wasn't going to be able to keep up with them anyway; I had been walking all day and didn't have a single ounce of energy left to give, not a fake smile to give—I had absolutely nothing left. Sometimes the stages of a spiritual awakening require us to reach the end of our rope, to exhaust all our coping mechanisms and defenses until we have no choice but to surrender to something greater than ourselves.

As my family began to disappear into the darkness, my pace became even slower, and that's when the conversation in my head became an actual conversation. It wasn't my itty-bitty shitty committee going full bore in my brain. There was a guest in there now. Whoever or whatever "it" was now began answering questions and subsequently asking them. "It" also didn't seem to plan on leaving me anytime soon. And so our verbal ping-pong match began going back and forth as I trudged down the sidewalk. The distinction between my usual internal chatter and this new voice was unmistakable. My regular mental dialogue was anxious, self-critical, and chaotic. This voice was calm, wise, and infinitely patient. It felt ancient and loving, like the voice of someone who had known me forever and loved me unconditionally. Something was about to shift in a way I'd never experienced before, and somehow, I knew it. The spiritual realm doesn't always announce itself with trumpets and lightning—sometimes it arrives in the quiet exhaustion of a man walking slowly behind his family, too tired to pretend anymore. And that's exactly when the most profound transformation of my life was about to begin.

Spiritual Summary

Sometimes your spiritual awakening begins in the most unlikely places—like walking slowly behind your family after a Disney movie, exhausted and disconnected from everything around you. When you're in crisis mode, physically and emotionally, that's often when your spiritual guides decide it's time to step in. The fact that you can't keep up with your family isn't just about being out of shape—in this case, it was the universe slowing me down so I could finally hear what's been trying to reach me. That "guest" in your head isn't your imagination or a breakdown; it's the beginning of a conversation that will change everything. Sometimes the most profound spiritual encounters happen when you're too tired to fight them off with logic and skepticism.

"In the Air Tonight":
When the Divine Intervenes
in Our Darkest Hour

The walk from the movie theater back to our hotel became the bridge between my old life and everything that would follow. Sometimes the most profound spiritual encounters happen not in sacred spaces or during meditation, but in the most ordinary moments when we're too depleted to maintain our usual defenses against the miraculous. This was my moment, though I didn't know it yet—the moment when everything would change.

"In the Air Tonight"
Phil Collins

I found myself walking toward the beach that night, Phil Collins's "In the Air Tonight" echoing in my mind. The song had always struck a chord inside of me, but that evening it felt prophetic. The lyrics seemed to anticipate the confrontation with truth that was about to unfold—not with another person, but with my own soul and with whatever force in the universe was about to intervene in my life. As I mentioned, music runs too deep in my life and my story to ignore. Legend has it that

Phil Collins tracked down someone who had wronged him, put him in the front row of his concert, and then performed that song, looking him dead in the eyes. I always loved that story. True or not, that night on the beach, I felt like the universe was about to do something similar to me, and there was no escaping it.

My internal conversation began with single words that triggered a series of cascading images, much like the phrase "a picture paints a thousand words," but in reverse. These images felt like going into warp speed for the first time on the Millennium Falcon. The sensation was disorienting and exhilarating simultaneously, as if my consciousness was being pulled into a different dimension of experience. The wind was picking up, carrying the light, stinging salt air to my nose. That unmistakable Florida-coast aroma you can taste on your lips, like lightly salted kettle chips. The sensory experience was more vivid than anything I'd felt in months. A chill ran down my neck and right arm. Not a full-body shiver, but the kind you get from an incredible song or a first kiss: part excitement, part joy, and part fear of not knowing what was going to happen next. This chill felt like a foreboding premonition—my body acknowledging that something significant was approaching.

I stopped at the crosswalk in front of the hotel and thought it would make the most sense to head on up to the room and get some rest, but instead of returning to the room, something else was telling me that it wasn't time to do that yet. It was as if it were eliminating that from my realm of possibilities and guiding me in a different direction—like a gentle push—to follow the sign pointing the way toward the beach. This guidance wasn't aggressive or pushy; it had the feel of a parent gently steering a child toward something wonderful they didn't yet know they needed to see. The feeling was unmistakable—I was being led, and for the first time in years, I trusted the leading more than my own exhausted analytical mind. I found a light post to lean against for a moment and took off my shoes and socks so I could feel the velvety sand on my feet. As I walked, the sand felt both warm and cool to the touch. The top layer was like a soft, warm blanket, but as my feet sank deeper, it became refreshingly cool, with a hint of dampness, like a cool cloth you'd place on your forehead to provide relief from a fever. This simple act of connecting with the earth became profoundly grounding. After days of being surrounded by concrete and artificial surfaces, feeling the natural texture of sand between my toes was like plugging into the earth's energy. It was the first moment of something real I'd felt in months. I continued walking toward the surf; it felt as though I was floating, and at nearly four hundred pounds, the sensation of floating was mildly foreign, and this felt electric, almost revitalizing. The contrast between my usual heavy, labored movement and this sense of weightless-ness gliding across the sand added to the surreal backdrop of the experience. Something was definitely happening to me, something beyond the physical realm.

As I got closer to the water, I stopped for a moment to take it all in. The mystery and power of the Gulf were bewitching to me, like the siren songs of a mermaid. Gentle, soothing, and inviting in one breath, and the power of God crashing down on you in the next breath—simply amazing. The gulf became a perfect metaphor for what I was experiencing: the gentle call of the divine followed by the overwhelming power of truth. White foam periodically broke the still, black water in the distance as waves made their way to the shoreline. The silky salt air now felt like a blanket over my entire body, and the taste shifted to something richer, like my Grandma Rinehart's gravy—basically a block of salt liquefied with brown food coloring.

I looked for a dry spot close enough to the water to take everything in without getting soaked. When I found the place, I started to squat down. I reached the point of no return and plopped down, flailing around like a turtle on its back before heaving myself upright. There was no one else around me at this point, so why did I care what I looked like? I don't know; I guess old habits die hard. My self-consciousness about my physical limitations remained, but perhaps that struggle to simply sit down was part of what I needed to experience—the humility, the surrender of trying to look dignified when dignity was impossible. There I sat, alone on the beach with no one visible as far as I could see, no lights—only the sounds, smell, and taste of the Gulf. It was amazing. But my mind had other plans. It didn't take long for the uninvited visitor in my head to make itself comfortable and start digging in. This wasn't the ethereal voice of James Earl Jones. This was my voice, yet again, it wasn't. My usual internal voice was snarky, negative, and downtrodden. This voice communicated with a fatherly maturity and understanding, with a more nurturing and curious, nonjudgmental tone. The distinction was so clear that even in my exhausted state, I immediately recognized I was no longer alone in my head.

Here's how the conversation unfolded:

Me: *I don't know what to do any longer. I feel like I've done all I can, but I still don't have any direction or answers.*

Voice: *"Lost? You know exactly where you are, don't you? And ... you aren't alone—you have your boys, and they love you."*

Me: *I know they love me, and Becky ... I love her, but I ... I ... Hell, I'm not sure I love myself, or much less like myself.*

Voice: "*Don't be ridiculous, you're a kind, loving, good—*"

Me: So! So what? What does that mean?! Kind . . . nice . . . good person, what?! Good father?! What?! It doesn't mean a thing. All it does is make me look weak and pathetic to someone I want so much to love me, and at this point, I don't know if anyone is better off with me around or not. My life insurance is paid up and I'm damn sure worth more dead than I am alive . . .

Voice: "**No!**"

Me: What do you mean, no? **I know** *for a fact I am.*

Voice: "**No!**"

Me: What, because you said so?

Voice: "No, Jim, that's not the answer. You have so much more to do, and this is not the end; this is where you start. That answer is not **your** *answer this time."*

The firmness of that "*no*" wasn't angry—it was absolute, like a loving but immovable force that would not allow me to continue down that path of thinking. It was the voice of someone who could see my future when I couldn't see past my present pain.

Me: Then what's the answer . . . this time? What's **my** *answer? I just feel . . . so . . . Please help me. Please?*

I was pleading, simply begging for the pain to stop.

Me: Please, God, please give me the strength to see things through to the end, whatever the outcome may be, whatever it looks like. I just need help, please, no more pain.

Voice: *"You're never alone; I am always with you. We are always with you."*

That simple statement changed everything. The "we" told me this wasn't just my imagination—this was communication from something larger, a collective of loving beings who had been watching over me all along, waiting for the moment when I was broken enough to finally listen. I felt a calm rush over me as I stared into the darkness of the Gulf. It wasn't weightlessness; it was more like someone hugging or maybe holding me. I was warm, my mind was quiet, and I was at peace. Peace—that ever-elusive feeling was something so foreign to me then, not having felt it in over a decade. It seemed like a lifetime ago. This peace wasn't the absence of problems—it was the presence of something far greater than my problems. It was the feeling of being held by an infinite love that knew every detail of my struggle and loved me not despite my flaws, but through them, with them, exactly who I was in that moment.

I don't know how long I sat in the stillness of that Florida night, but there I sat, breathing, listening, soaking up the feeling of whatever had wrapped its arms around me. I felt a knowing I couldn't describe, like I had faith that I would be good again, that my entire life would be good again. This wasn't my imagination or wishful thinking—this was soul-deep knowledge downloaded directly from the heavens, maybe even from God. As my mind drifted off, it wasn't filled with the usual negative chatter I'd grown accustomed to. There was no "you're fat and pathetic, no wonder your wife doesn't want to be with you any longer." There was nothing—no voice, no negativity, just peace, and I loved it. The peaceful silence was broken by that voice again:

Voice: *"You will not see another birthday in your current state. Your happiness comes from within. I am within. You'll find joy and contentment in new ways, in ways you never knew before."*

Each of these statements arrived with the weight of prophecy, not as threats but as loving promises and not-yet-realized truths. The message was clear: Change was not optional, it was inevitable, and it would be guided by something far wiser and greater than my conscious mind. It felt almost biblical, but there was no burning bush, no lightning, no thunder rumbling; it was just me, alone on the beach in perfect, pitch-black stillness. The divine doesn't always announce itself with dramatic special effects—sometimes it whispers truth into our hearts when we're finally quiet enough to listen. Everything had slowed down while I sat on the beach. My mind slowed down, which was a miracle in itself. My breathing slowed to the point where I could barely tell if I was still breathing at all. It was as if I no longer needed to breathe, as if I were underwater or in outer space. Each breath was suspended in an eternity of comfort, warmth, and peace. I hadn't felt this good in . . . hell, I couldn't honestly remember ever feeling this good. Before I could ask another question, an answer came:

Voice: *"You'll know what to do, you will have the answers. Now go and rest—the beginning is near."*

My suspended animation came to an abrupt end, like someone had shaken me awake. Holy shit, what time is it? I had no idea. My phone was in the room, plugged into the charger, dead from the day's events. I hadn't needed it—my family was with me, so I'd left it behind in the room. Even as it happened, part of me wondered if I was losing my mind. The rational voice in my head was telling me that none of this made sense. But the peace . . . the peace I felt was undeniably real. The transformation in my internal state was so dramatic that no amount of logical skepticism could dismiss it. For now, my focus needed to be on getting back to the hotel room without waking anyone. The return to practical reality after such a profound spiritual experience created its own form of cognitive dissonance—how do you go from conversing with who knows, the Divine Spirit, God, to sneaking into a hotel room? The hotel lobby was dimly lit, just enough to guide me to the elevators. Without the usual crowd of vacationers, the elevator seemed unusually loud. I opened our door quietly and attempted my best *Mission: Impossible* entrance, though it probably resembled Chris Farley in *Tommy Boy* more than Tom Cruise. I crept toward the bedroom and managed to enter without waking my wife. That lasted until I slipped into bed. At nearly four hundred pounds, stealth isn't much of an option—the freaking mattress betrayed me immediately. "Are you just getting to bed?"

"Yeah. Sorry, I didn't mean to wake you."

Groggily, she reached for her watch. "It's 3:13! In the morning!"

"Yeah, sorry, I just lost track of time. Try to go back to sleep." A couple of profanity-laced murmurs later, she was asleep again.

I lay wide awake, replaying what had just happened. Did I fall asleep and dream all of that? I must have—I was tired after all, and it was definitely late. I spent the next several minutes trying to rationalize the experience until I finally nodded off. But deep down, I knew it wasn't a dream. The feelings I had, those were real; they weren't made up. The answers to questions that I had yet to ask: How in the hell could that be a dream? Something had shifted within me, deep inside of me, in my soul. Something, I wasn't sure what it was exactly, but something had begun. The distinction between this experience and any dream I'd ever had was unmistakable. This beach experience would become the pivot point between who I had been and who I was about to become. Dreams fade when you wake up—this experience had burned itself into my consciousness with the intensity of an actual memory. The peace I felt was still there, the knowing was still there, and deep inside, I understood that my life would never be the same.

"Under the Pale Moon Glow"
Jim Alstott

Spiritual Summary

Sometimes, when you're at your absolute lowest, when suicide feels like the best or logical solution, that's precisely when the universe can step in with its strongest intervention. The voice that speaks to you in your darkest hour isn't your depression or your fear—it's your soul, your guides, your higher self, reminding you that your current state isn't permanent. When that voice says, "This is not your answer," listen. When it promises that happiness comes from within and that you'll find joy in ways you never knew before, trust it. A spiritual awakening often begins in the darkness, when you're most vulnerable, when you're broken enough to finally hear what's been trying to reach you all along. That peace you feel, that's real. That knowing, that voice telling you that something's about to change. Hold on to that knowledge and believe in it, because it *is* coming from your soul, God, or spirit; it's a divine message intended to be heard by you.

"I Still Haven't Found What I'm Looking For":
The Seeking Stage

The morning after my beach encounter with the divine, I woke up feeling different. Not dramatically transformed—I was still nearly four hundred pounds, still in a wobbly marriage, still facing all the same external problems. But something fundamental had shifted inside me. That voice on the beach had planted a seed of hope where only despair had lived, and now that seed was demanding to grow. The question was what the hell was I supposed to do with it?

"I Still Haven't Found What I'm Looking For"
U2

You know that feeling you get when you're searching for your car keys and they're right there in your hand? That's kind of what U2 was getting at with "I Still Haven't Found What I'm Looking For," except they're talking about God and true life meaning and all that heavy stuff that, if you're anything like me, keeps you up until three in the morning searching for answers on the internet instead of sleeping. Here's the thing that sticks with me about this song: When I really started paying attention to it, Bono's basically saying, "Yeah, I believe

41

in Jesus, I've climbed the highest mountains, I've run through fields, hell, I've scaled city walls . . . and I'm still looking for something more." This resonated inside me on a level that surprised me, because it perfectly captured the paradox of spiritual awakening—the more you discover, the more you realize there is to discover.

Most church folks, like my dad, would lose their shit hearing something like that. Growing up, if you had faith, that was supposed to be the end of the story. Problem solved, case closed, see you Sunday morning. But Bono's out here saying faith and searching aren't opposites—they're dance partners, and that's what I had to come to grips with. I believe in God, and I think that God would be okay with me saying I'm spiritual, instead of saying I'm religious. My buddy Ken explained it in one of the easiest-to-understand ways I've heard. Ken says that religion is for groups of people or gatherings of people, often driven by ego and comparison, whereas spirituality is internal. This distinction became crucial for me—it gave me permission to seek truth without feeling like I was betraying my foundational beliefs. So, like Bono, I set out to find what I was looking for, but I had to do it in my own way, following my own path rather than the prescribed route I'd been taught was the only valid one.

My seeking began in an unorthodox way. It started with a conversation I had with an old high school friend who shared the monumental shifts she experienced in her life when meditation and another practice, reiki, appeared in her life. Sometimes the universe sends us exactly the person we need to hear from at exactly the right time, and my friend Lynn turned out to be that person for me. Lynn told me about feeling trapped, like a prisoner in a torture chamber, with thoughts that wouldn't leave her mind. She said she felt like she was in an endless loop of agony and depression and couldn't find her way out, until she found the meditations and coursework of Ms. Kelly Schwegel. Her description of her mental state was so similar to mine that it was like looking in a mirror—finally, someone who understood the particular hell of living inside an anxious, self-critical mind.

I explained where I was currently in my life to Lynn, and as we talked, I felt at ease, as if Kelly Schwegel was supposed to help me find answers to some of my questions. This feeling of "supposed to" became a recurring theme in my spiritual journey—the sense that certain people, practices, and experiences were divinely orchestrated rather than coincidental. Lynn was kind enough to send along a couple of Kelly's meditations so that I could try this meditation thing on for size. I also confided to Lynn that I was skeptical as to whether I would be able to quiet my adult-ADHD mind long enough to get through a meditation. She said she had the perfect guided meditation to help me calm the internal chatter of my mind, which is routinely distracted by shiny objects. She sent over the Pineal Gland Activation meditation. Who would have known this meditation thing had so many rhymes? This new thing—thousands-of-years-old thing for others—meditation, was intriguing to me, but first, what the hell is the pineal gland? This is where my seeking, a.k.a. going down a spiritual rabbit hole, began.

Spiritual Summary

Faith and seeking aren't opposites at all; in fact, they're dance partners. Anyone who tells you that believing means you stop asking questions has confused spirituality with obedience. The universe has a way of putting exactly the right person in your path at precisely the right moment, and your job is to recognize them when they show up and trust your intuition enough to follow where they lead. Your awakening doesn't have to look like anyone else's, either. The rabbit hole you're supposed to go down might start with a high school friend and a meditation with a mantra you've never heard of. The seeking stage is where curiosity becomes your compass, and every question you ask opens a door you didn't even know existed.

The Pineal Gland:
That Little Weird Thing in Your Head

The journey from beach awakening to understanding the spiritual mechanics of consciousness led me down some fascinating rabbit holes. One of the most intriguing was learning about a tiny organ in my head I'd never heard of but that might hold the key to understanding spiritual experiences. There's this miniature pine cone–shaped thing sitting smack dab in the middle of your brain that's been driving spiritual folks batshit crazy for centuries. It's called the pineal gland, and for something about the size of a grain of rice, it sure knows how to stir up some serious metaphysical drama.

Where in the hell is this thing? Picture cracking open your skull like a walnut (don't actually do this, obviously), and right there in the center, tucked between the two halves of your brain is a biological Cracker Jack prize. That's your pineal gland, chilling out in what brain scientists call the epithalamus. What's weird is that most stuff in your brain comes in pairs—left this, right that—but the pineal gland is all by its lonesome right down the middle. This little thing has to be special, because there's only one pineal, not a left or right pineal. The singularity of this gland has fascinated researchers and mystics alike . . . why would nature create only one of something unless it served a unique and important function?

What does this little thing actually do? From a straight-up scientific perspective, your pineal gland is basically running your internal clock. It pumps out melatonin, which is the chemical that makes you want to face-plant right into your pillow when it gets dark. Think of it as your body's Sandman, the thing that knows when it's bedtime without you having to check your phone. Here's where it gets interesting—this thing has light-sensitive cells in it. Light-sensitive cells. In the middle of your brain where no light should ever reach. It's like having eyeballs inside your skull, which is either really cool or really creepy, depending on how you look at it. And get this—scientists have found that it also produces tiny amounts of DMT in rodents (we're still waiting for proof in humans). Yeah . . . that DMT. The thing they call "the spirit molecule." More on that mind-bending detail in a minute.

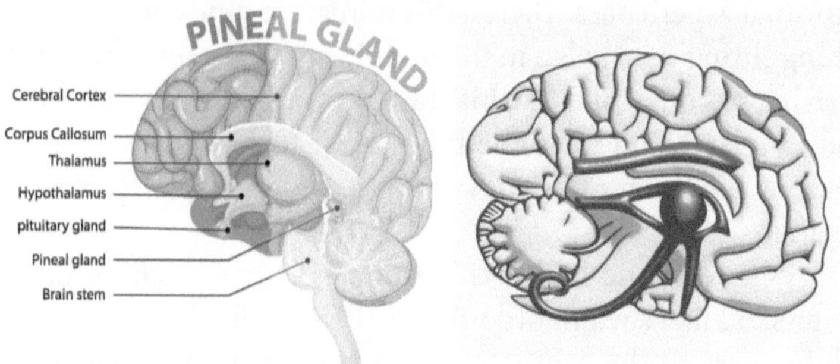

This is all so cool. The pineal gland is a spiritual heavy hitter. For thousands of years, people have referred to this small gland as everything from "the seat of the soul" to "the third eye" to "your personal hotline to God." The ancient Egyptians were obsessed with it. They thought it was the Eye of Horus, your direct connection between this world and whatever the hell is out there beyond it. Hindu and Buddhist folks have been talking about the third-eye chakra—located right where the pineal gland sits—as the center of intuition and spiritual insight for ages. You know that feeling when you just know something, but you can't explain how? When you get that gut feeling about a person or situation that turns out to be dead-on accurate? A lot of spiritual experts say that's your pineal gland talking. The DMT bomb is where things get off the rails a bit, maybe not as wild as my friend Gail Alexander's description of her spiritual awakening—"It was like being on Mr. Toad's Wild Ride on acid"—but trippy, nonetheless. Remember how I mentioned this thing maybe produces DMT? Well, some researchers think that during near-death experiences, deep meditation, or other mystical states, your pineal gland might pump out a bigger load of this naturally occurring psychedelic chemical into your system. That could explain those radical spiritual experiences people have—the out-of-body stuff, seeing dead relatives, getting downloads of universal knowledge, all that heavy stuff that can freak the hell out of someone. Your own brain might be producing its proprietary version of ayahuasca right there in your head. Holy shit, right? Right?!

This possibility completely reframed how I understood my beach experience. Maybe that profound peace and the voice I heard weren't external phenomena—maybe they were the result of my pineal gland finally activating after years of being suppressed by stress, poor health, and disconnection from my spiritual nature.

A modern conspiracy—and who doesn't love a good conspiracy theory? Some people believe that fluoride in water, processed food, and all the artificial light we're constantly exposed to are calcifying our pineal glands, essentially turning it into a little rock instead of a functioning spiritual antenna that can broadcast out into the cosmos. I'm not sure if there's some grand conspiracy to cut us off from our spiritual mojo, but I do know that our modern lifestyle is pretty far removed from how humans lived for most of history. Maybe there's something to that. I dunno.

How do you work with this thing? Look, I'm not gonna tell you what to believe, but if you're curious about activating or working with your pineal gland, here's what people say works: Spend time in complete darkness. Meditate with your eyes closed. Some folks swear by basking in the glow of natural sunlight at sunrise and sunset, while equipped with proper safety eyewear. Others try to clean up their diets, avoid the overuse of chemical fluoride, and cut back on exposure to artificial light at night. Will any of this turn you into some kind of psychic superhero? Beats the hell out of me. But it can't hurt to take better care of your body and your brain, right?

The bottom line here is this: I remember that voice in my head that told me to go to the closet in my bedroom when I was four, then later instructed me to open the door and suggested I take a look inside. Was that my pineal gland talking? Some kind of spiritual intuition? Random coincidence? I honestly don't know, and maybe it's okay not knowing for now. What I do know is that this tiny little gland sits right at the crossroads of science and spirituality, pumping out sleep hormones by day and possibly spirit molecules by night. Maybe the ancient mystics were onto something when they referred to it as the gateway to higher consciousness. Or maybe it's just another organ doing its job. I'll leave that up to you to decide. Either way, there's still so much mystery packed into that three-pound universe between your ears. I'm reasonably certain that scientists and spiritualists will be busy for years to come trying to figure it all out. And that mystery was about to become my new obsession as I dove deeper into understanding the connection between consciousness and spiritual awakening.

Spiritual Summary

Your pineal gland just might be your body's built-in spiritual antenna, or it might just be keeping your sleep schedule on track. The truth is probably somewhere in the middle. But that little pine cone in your head has been considered sacred across several cultures for thousands of years, and it's still producing compounds that can alter consciousness. Sometimes the most profound spiritual experiences come from the most unexpected places—including a grain-of-rice-sized gland you probably never knew you had. Trust your intuition, pay attention to those inexplicable moments of knowing, and remember that the veil between science and spirit might be thinner than we think.

"Waiting for a Girl Like You":
Finding My First Spiritual Teacher

The transition from learning about the pineal gland to finding someone who could help me understand these spiritual concepts in practical terms shows how the universe orchestrates exactly the right connections at exactly the right time. After weeks of trying to meditate on my own and feeling like I was getting nowhere, the universe decided it was time to introduce me to the teacher I needed.

"Waiting for a Girl Like You"
Foreigner

"Waiting for a Girl Like You" is a power ballad released by the band Foreigner back in 1981. The lyrics of the song can certainly be considered a love song, but for me, it was a different kind of love; this was more like a bolt of lightning to the forehead—a spiritual sort of love. Little did I know, this was the beginning of a transformation; this transformative relationship was to be the catalyst for my spiritual growth and enlightenment. While the song speaks to waiting for the right person, in my case, it wasn't a new love interest I was waiting for, but rather a more spiritual relationship, where a teacher, guide, or mentor comes into our lives when we are ready to receive their wisdom. For me, the timing was divinely orchestrated. The song's message echoed the idea of meeting someone willing to share a deep spiritual connection, making the learning process more profound and meaningful. Lynn and I had several conversations over the next few weeks, as my curiosity and interest in knowing more escalated into a mild obsession. It got to the point where Lynn thought it best that I go straight to the source of this information and speak with Kelly Schwegel myself. Lynn set up a meeting on my behalf to provide a warm introduction, and two days later, I found myself on a Zoom call with none other than Ms. Kelly Schwegel. The anticipation I felt before that first call was unlike anything I'd felt in a while. It wasn't like the nervousness that would hit you right before you walked on stage for a performance, exactly—it was more like the feeling you get before meeting someone you instinctively know will change your life, even though you've never met them before.

Kelly's credentials, symposia, and talks are impressive, so I thought you might appreciate learning a little more about her. Kelly Schwegel has earned an undergraduate degree in education, a master's degree in educational administration, and an educational specialist degree in educational leadership, holding teaching, principal, director of special education, and superintendent certifications. After working in the field of education for twenty years, she left to follow her calling to train, speak, and heal in the area of spirituality and the natural healing arts. She became a reiki master instructor in 2011 and has taught countless individuals to heal themselves and intuitively guide others along their own personal healing journey. She has spent several years researching and working in the metaphysical world and is a fantastic speaker.

Kelly has dozens of videos on YouTube, and I've included a link to make it easy to explore what Kelly has to offer: youtube.com/@KellySchwegel/videos.

What struck me about Kelly's background was how it mirrored my own journey in some ways—the transition from a conventional career to following a spiritual calling. Her educational background gave her the ability to explain complex spiritual concepts in ways that were both accessible and scientifically grounded, which was exactly what my skeptical mind needed. My first Zoom call with Kelly lasted nearly two hours, which was much longer than she had intended, but there was so much to cover, and I was like a kid in a candy store. I couldn't get enough information, and the questions just kept flowing out of me like a river. The conversation felt effortless and natural, as if we'd known each other for years rather than having just met. Near the end of our conversation, Kelly suggested that I watch some of her videos and get comfortable with the information, and suggested we schedule another time to connect in two weeks, which is precisely what we did. Kelly and I met every couple of weeks for months, at which time I realized that she was much more than an educator. Kelly was becoming my first spiritual mentor.

The relationship that developed with Kelly was unlike any I'd had before. It wasn't just teacher-student—it was more like a spiritual family member helping another family member remember who they really were. She had the rare gift of meeting people exactly where they were in their spiritual journey while gently encouraging them to take the next step. We were discussing things on both an esoteric and a scientific level. This is what drew me in and made a deep connection with me. What Kelly was saying wasn't just some mumbo-jumbo, woo-woo crap; she supported her statements with scientific studies and findings that narrowed the chasm of skepticism for me. This balance between spiritual wisdom and scientific validation became the bridge that allowed my rational mind to accept what my soul already knew to be true. When I asked her about going through the reiki certification training, a type of energy healing practice, Kelly felt I was ready to take the next step in my spiritual adventure. As our routine had already been established for meeting every couple of weeks, I started the coursework to become a holistic reiki 1 practitioner two weeks later. Okay, moment of truth here. I am the type of person who jumps into the pool with a cannonball entry; I'm not a toe-dipper. So, of course, I immediately continued with the coursework and became certified in holistic reiki 2 and 3, and then went on to receive my holistic reiki master 1 and 2 certifications (qualifying me to teach reiki), but what in the hell was I going to do with it?

I didn't necessarily want to drop everything and be this great healer of people; I just had a curiosity that was so extreme, I couldn't get enough of this spiritual curriculum. The hunger for knowledge was insatiable—each answer led to ten more questions; each technique I learned opened doors to deeper understanding. I will say that my sons—well, at least one of my sons, my middle son—and my dog benefited from my teachings. Believe it or not, animals are said to love the healing energies that reiki provides, but my dog, on the other hand, did not. She couldn't get away fast enough the first time I used reiki on her; she totally freaked out and ran away. That is, until she experienced reiki again and again. Roxy, my Rottweiler, soon began to almost ask for her healing sessions. She would push up against my leg, plop down on the floor, roll over on her back, and just stare at me until I would assume my position on the floor near her and commence with the reiki magic. Watching this transformation in Roxy was one of my first concrete validations that something real was happening with this energy work—animals don't pretend or placebo effect themselves into feeling better.

Spiritual Summary

Kelly is a wonderful example of how it's never too late to change direction in your life and follow your passion. When you're ready for a teacher, the universe will drop one in your lap, or in a Zoom call. Your job is to recognize them and dive in with a cannonball, not to stand on the edge, dipping your toe in the water. The right spiritual mentor won't just feed you woo-woo sprinkled with tofu; they'll bridge the gap between what your soul already knows and what your skeptical mind needs to hear, backing up the mystical with the scientific until even the most stubborn part of you must admit something real is happening. And sometimes your best validation comes from unexpected places, like a Rottweiler who can't fake a placebo effect rolling over and demanding her healing session. When the student is ready, the teacher appears, and if you're lucky, that teacher becomes family.

Mr. Miyagi Magic:
Wax-On, Wax-Off Reiki

Since I'd thrown myself headfirst into reiki training, I figure I should probably explain what it actually is for those who might be wondering if I completely lost my mind. The journey from skeptic to practitioner had been pretty quick, and now I find myself in the position of trying to explain something that sounds completely bananas to the rational mind. Reiki is a Japanese healing technique in which people place their hands on you (or near you), claiming they're channeling universal life energy to help heal whatever is wrong with you. Depending on who you ask, it's either complete bullshit or the most powerful healing modality on the planet. I've experienced both sides of this coin. I think there are a lot of variables involved, but my overall impression of reiki is that it's a powerful tool that can be used to help many. The effectiveness often depends on the practitioner's training, intention, and connection to the energy, as well as the recipient's openness to receiving healing. The whole thing was developed by a Japanese gentleman named Mikao Usui in the 1920s following a spiritual awakening on a mountain. But, of course, it happened on a mountain. Everything happens on a mountain. Why does the prerequisite for having a spiritual breakthrough have to happen on a mountain? I live in Illinois. Where am I going to find a mountain? So, maybe if you don't live near a mountain, we can find a place without the mountainous incline that will work. If you are near a mountain, then you're all set. The good news is that spiritual awakening can happen anywhere—beaches in Florida work just fine, as I can personally attest.

Reiki comes from two Japanese words: *rei* (universal) and *ki* (life energy). So, basically, it's "universal life energy." The idea is that there's this invisible energy flowing through everything—you, me, your annoying neighbor, that houseplant you keep forgetting to water—and when that energy gets blocked or out of whack, you get sick or feel off. Think of a reiki practitioner as being a set of human jumper cables, channeling this universal energy through their hands into your body to get things flowing again. They don't use their own energy, but universal energies, as they're just the conduit for whatever energies flow in cosmically.

There are different levels of reiki training—level 1, level 2, and master level—where you learn different symbols and techniques. Some people can perform distance reiki, where they send you healing energy from across the country while you're sitting on your couch in your pajamas. The distance healing aspect was particularly intriguing to me—if energy isn't bound by physical proximity, it suggests we're all connected in ways that defy our usual understanding of space and time. From a spiritual perspective, reiki is based on some pretty fundamental ideas that show up across several traditions: that we're all connected by invisible energy, that healing happens when energy flows freely, that intention matters as much as technique, and that love is the ultimate healing force. Whether reiki works because it's channeling actual universal energy, or because it gives people permission to slow down and receive caring attention, or because the placebo effect is more powerful than we realize—honestly, I don't care anymore.

What matters is that people consistently report feeling better after sessions, more peaceful, less anxious, and sometimes even physically improved.

My experience with reiki opened my mind to possibilities I'd never considered and gave me my first taste of consciously working with energy for healing purposes. It was the perfect introduction to energy work for someone like me who needed both the spiritual experience and the structured learning approach to make sense of it all. And it prepared me perfectly for the questioning stage that was about to explode in my consciousness.

Spiritual Summary

Reiki may be channeling actual universal energy, or it may be the power of human intention and touch dressed up in spiritual language. The truth is probably somewhere in between. What matters is that it gives people permission to slow down, receive care, and believe in their body's ability to heal. Sometimes the most profound healing happens not because we can explain it, but because we're open enough to let it in. Trust your experience over anyone else's opinion, including mine. If it feels healing to you, then it probably is.

"What's Going On":
When Everything You Believed Gets Questioned

The progression from finding my first spiritual teacher to questioning literally everything I'd ever been taught about reality was both exciting and terrifying. Learning about energy healing and ancient spiritual practices through Kelly's guidance had opened a door, but what lay beyond that door was a complete deconstruction of the worldview I'd spent fifty-plus years building. It's one thing to accept that energy healing might be real; it's another thing entirely to realize if that's true, then what else have you been wrong about? Before I get much further along, I think it's important to point out that each of us has our own unique version of the stages of spiritual awakening. I know I mentioned it previously, but I felt it was a good time to say it again, because mine had stages that melded into one, such as stages three and four, in this instance.

"What's Going On?"

Marvin Gaye

Marvin Gaye was on to something when he asked the question that reverberates down the hall of every spiritual awakening: "What's Going On?" That's exactly how I felt when I began the following stages of my spiritual awakening. My brain was on "Big Train Don't Stop" mode, because once you start having spiritual experiences, that's exactly what your brain starts looking for, almost demanding to know about literally everything you've ever believed about your reality. The shift from passive acceptance to active questioning wasn't gradual—it was like someone had flipped a switch in my brain. Suddenly, every "truth" I'd been handed seemed questionable, every assumption worth taking a closer look at, every belief system worth investigating. It was simultaneously liberating and overwhelming as hell.

I look back on the lockdown during the pandemic somewhat fondly. It was during this time in our history that I had the opportunity to delve into our past, examine what is accepted in our society, and reflect on my own belief system. While some may have enjoyed virtual happy hours or virtual cooking classes, I was deeply immersed in interrogating my belief system and why I felt or thought about things the way I did. The pandemic created an unexpected gift of time and isolation that forced many of us to confront ourselves without the usual everyday distractions of our lives. For people in the midst of spiritual awakening, this period became an intensive retreat into self-examination that might have taken years to accomplish under normal circumstances. You might think of it as your accelerated course on woo-woo.

So this is where things start to get really fun—well, maybe not so much fun, I should say, freaking exhausting. Imagine being a toddler again, except instead of asking "Why?" about why the sky is blue, you're asking "Why?" about why you've spent fifty-something years accepting that this is just how life works and how life is supposed to be. What came to mind repeatedly for me during this stage was a phrase my dad used regularly: "Jimbo, the only thing you *have* to do is pay taxes and die." What in the—? Pay taxes and die?! What?! What about . . . ? What about not going along with things just because you were told, "because I said so." I couldn't stop asking questions, and I was questioning freaking everything. Why do we live the way we live? Why do we accept that we have to work jobs we don't enjoy, just to pay for shit that we don't really need? Why *don't* we talk about spiritual experiences like they're normal? Why did nobody tell me I had a pea-sized thing in my brain that might be my personal Bat Phone to the universe? So many questions . . . so many answers . . . that just led to more questions. The questioning became compulsive, almost addictive. Each answer I discovered opened ten more doors, revealed ten more mysteries, challenged ten more assumptions I didn't even know I was making. It was like being a spiritual detective in a case where every piece of evidence made the mystery more profound, rather than clearer. The problem is, once you start pulling on these threads, the whole scratchy wool sweater of your worldview starts unraveling. And let me tell you, standing there in your freak-flag spiritual underwear, wondering what the hell you actually believe can be both liberating and terrifying as hell. You start feeling a bit like Pink Floyd's "Comfortably Numb"—but instead of being comfortably numb, you're uncomfortably awake to everything you've been sleepwalking through to this point in your life.

"Comfortably Numb"
Pink Floyd

This awakening to how much of life I'd been experiencing on autopilot was alarming. It was like realizing I'd been watching a movie of my life instead of actually living it, and now suddenly I was thrust into the director's chair without knowing how to work the camera. You start questioning the beliefs your family so carefully bestowed upon you, the stuff society told you was "just the way things are" or "we've always done it this way; don't question it," and even the things you learned in school that seemed like facts that were carved in stone—maybe those weren't facts at all. Maybe they were just someone's opinions that got repeated generation after generation, until they became accepted as truths. When you think of it that way, it seems like the way urban legends get started. One person freaks out, makes up a plausible story, says it with conviction, and there you have it—it's doctrine now . . . or is it? This realization that so much of what I'd accepted as "truth" was actually a bunch of collective agreements masquerading as facts was, quite honestly, scary as fuck. If these "truths" weren't actually true, then what else had I been wrong about? What other possibilities had I dismissed without investigating? After you've questioned everything outside of yourself, it's now time for you to set your sights on that person in the mirror. And so you inevitably start questioning yourself. And I'm not just talking the "Am I a good person?" kind of questioning. I'm talking about "Who the hell am I once I strip away the layers of the person I've been told I should be?" That kind of questioning.

The first truly honest question I asked myself was "What happened to you? Why did you decide to give up on yourself, your happiness, your excitement, and zest for life?" Don't get me wrong—I love my kids and my wife, I honestly do—but I didn't like myself, not at all. I must have hated myself to intentionally sabotage my health. I mean, think about it . . . I ballooned up to nearly four hundred pounds, and that isn't an exaggeration either. I was attempting to dull the pain of having to be me by self-medicating with pain meds and booze. I don't really know when I stopped asking what happened and started asking why things happened. What was the root cause behind all of these actions? These were very deliberate choices I had been making up until now; it's as if I were playing a game of chicken with death and myself, or Russian roulette, but instead of a gun, my weapon of choice was a big glass of rum, a splash of diet soda (kind of ironic I was drinking diet soda and weighed as much as an adolescent bull), and pain medication. Did I have a death wish? The disturbing answer was yes. I didn't verbalize it, mind you, but through my actions, I was fucking screaming it from the top of the mountain. But what was it? The truth was, I didn't resemble the picture that had been painted for me . . . and by me, and I was in pain. I was in pain because I couldn't live up to what I had pictured as amounting to a successful life, so I added protective layers. My fat that I built up over several years had become my emotional and spiritual Kevlar. The authentic me was buried beneath hundreds of pounds, and that's when it came to me. This was it: I no longer hated myself, nor did I feel sorry for myself. This was the time when I regained control of my metaphysical steering wheel and charted the course I'm still sailing on today.

When I look back now, it was as if I started peeling back layers of myself like an onion; each layer revealed something I forgot was there, much like the smoke and mirrors of the Wizard in the movie *The Wizard of Oz*. The crying part from the peeling of the onions was real for me—not just occasional tears, but deep, cathartic sobbing as layers of suppressed emotion and forgotten dreams came to the surface. Each layer I peeled back revealed another version of myself I'd abandoned along the way to become who I thought I was supposed to be. You realize that most of what you think of as being "you" is actually just a collection of roles, or masks that you've worn to portray a particular part you've been cast to play. I've played the good son, the responsible father, the reliable employee, and countless others. But underneath all those costumes, there's this person you hardly know anymore or even recognize. Maybe what's left is a person you never really knew to begin with. I started asking myself questions I'd never thought to ask before: What do I actually want? Not what I'm supposed to want. Not what someone else said I should want. What makes me happy when nobody's watching me and nobody's judging me? What lights up my soul? Which parts of my personality did I hide away because they didn't fit the acceptable mold?

These questions were revolutionary for someone who'd spent decades being the person others expected me to be. The idea that I could choose what I wanted, rather than figuring out what was expected and delivering that, was amazing. It's like doing an archaeological dig on your soul. You're digging through all the stuff that got piled on top of who you really are. Layer after layer of patterns and beliefs, and this stuff isn't just your stuff; it's generational stuff. It's your parents' stuff, their parents' stuff, and so on. Oh, and if you happen to be in a relationship with someone else, it just adds an additional multiplier to things, because now you have the gift of adding that person's "stuff" and their parent's "stuff," and so on. It's the predetermined expectations, fears, and other people's opinions, as well as cultural programming; all the while, you're just trying to find the authentic *you* buried underneath it all. The generational aspect of this digging was particularly intense. I began to see how patterns of behavior, belief systems, and even fears had been passed down through my family line like some kind of invisible inheritance. Breaking free from these patterns meant not just changing myself, but interrupting cycles that had been running for generations.

This whole process feels like being a detective in your own life, except every piece of evidence you find makes the case more complicated instead of clearer. But here's the thing—you can't stop. Once you start questioning, it's like you're gaining spiritual momentum. You're committed to finding out what's actually real, even if it means discovering that half of what you thought was real was just conditioning and outdated beliefs. Sometimes what you find surprises the shit out of you. Maybe you discover you're way more intuitive than you thought.

When I was young, I was diagnosed with severe allergies. I'm talking *crazy* allergies—looking back, I'm shocked my parents weren't told I was allergic to air, my own face, or the color blue. We're talking the whole alphabet of allergies here. So most of my childhood involved weekly treks to the allergist's office, where I'd get pumped full of shots and then had to sit around for the next hour like a ticking allergic time bomb, just to make sure I didn't go into anaphylactic shock on the way home. And if I were lucky enough to receive the old gamma globulin shot? Holy hell. A gamma globulin shot is essentially like getting injected with the concentrated snot of a thousand strangers. (You're welcome for that visual.) When I had one of those bad boys, we'd be parked in the allergist's office for at least ninety minutes, my mom watching me like I might spontaneously combust at any moment.

So there we were, week after week, year after year, trying to pass the time. We played all the classic games: Hangman, Tic-Tac-Toe, and "Let's see how many ceiling tiles have water stains." But then my mom introduced a different game that would change everything, though I didn't know it at the time. "I'm thinking of a number between one and ten," she'd say. "What is it?" And I'd guess. Here's the weird part—I was freaking fantastic at it. Like, scary good. We played it over and over, gradually widening the gap between the numbers. One to twenty. One to fifty. One to two hundred. And I kept nailing it. Not every time, but way more than the law of averages would suggest. I received allergy shots from kindergarten until the middle of eighth grade. That's like eight years of sitting in waiting rooms, eight years of this guessing game. We got so proficient that we started adding complexities. Colors. Words. Animals. Eventually, we were doing short sentences.

"I'm thinking of something," she'd say, and I'd respond with "blue elephant wearing sandals," and she'd look at me like I'd just pulled a rabbit out of a hat because that's precisely what she was thinking. I'm sure you've figured out where this is going, right? Because until recently, and I mean, embarrassingly recently, I hadn't given much thought to our little waiting room game. It was just something we did, like breathing or complaining about traffic. But holy shit, what we were doing was *telepathy*. Actual, honest-to-God, science-can-kiss-my-ass telepathy. Before the science police come knocking, let me be clear: I don't give a shit that there's "not enough empirical evidence" to support telepathic communication. It happened. It happened *a lot*. You know what else science couldn't explain for a long time? Bumblebees flying. It was considered a scientific improbability for the insect to create enough lift to fly, but those buzzing bastards kept doing it anyway.

Telepathy, for those keeping score at home, is defined as the communication or transfer of information that bypasses traditional mediums, such as speech, writing, or interpretive dance—just a pure mind-to-mind connection. And you know what? N.W.A had the right idea with "Fuck tha Police"—except in this case, it's "Fuck tha Science Police." (Shout-out to N.W.A, Ice Cube, and Dr. Dre for that timeless classic about questioning authority, which I'm now applying to paranormal phenomena because that's how my brain works). While writing this book, I've been slowly discovering just how similar my mom and I really were. It's like finding out you've been wearing your dad's old concert t-shirt for years without knowing he was actually at Woodstock. This revelation is filling in massive gaps, connecting dots I didn't even know existed. My mom had these gifts, and I mean, *had* to have had them. But she was born in the 1940s—can you imagine trying to explain telepathic abilities in the era of *Father Knows Best* and casserole recipes? It would've been like the Salem witch trials meets *Ozzie and Harriet*, or for most of us, *Friends*. She did what any of us would do: She hid them, pushed them down, treated them like a shameful secret instead of the incredible gifts they were. And honestly? It's not much different today. Hell, if someone had told me ten years ago that I'd be writing about telepathic connections with my dead mother, I probably would've slowly backed away while maintaining eye contact and reaching for my phone to call for help.

What if those long hours in the allergist's office weren't just about treating my allergies? What if my mom were secretly training me? What if every guess-the-number game was actually her way of saying, "Hey, kid, you've got the gift too, and I'm going to help you develop it in the only way I can without anyone thinking we're completely insane"? Wow, that sounded pretty *X-Filey*. Because let's be real: "We're going to the allergist to develop our telepathic abilities" doesn't exactly fly with the PTA crowd, let alone my dad. Holy shit, don't let me go down that rabbit hole! "We're going to the allergist because Jimmer's allergic to everything, including his own shadow"? Now, that's totally acceptable. I'm beginning to think my mom was a genius. A secret telepathic genius disguised as a suburban mom just trying to keep her kid from dying via dog dander exposure. And now, years later,

I'm finally understanding that those weren't just games, they were lessons. Secret training sessions from Professor Charles Xavier's *X-Men* academy, but mine were taking place in an allergist's waiting room.

So here I am at fifty-nine, playing Inspector Clouseau (a cool *Pink Panther* reference for you) with my own spiritual awakening, except my magnifying glass is my third eye, which works about as well as trying to read fine print after three margaritas on some days. I'm putting together all the pieces from my life's journey: The signs, symbols, synchronicities, occurrences, and those conversations that made no sense at the time, but now, most of the time anyway, are crystal freaking clear. It's like trying to glue a treasure map back together that's been ripped into a thousand pieces, half of them missing, and the most important bits are stuck under a pile of Doritos on the carpet I haven't vacuumed since 2019. The epiphanies keep coming . . . *Pop!* There's a connection! *Bang!* Oh, that's what that meant!

If you've experienced this process, you're nodding right now, maybe laughing, or perhaps even crying, because you know *exactly* what I'm talking about. And if you haven't? Well, you're in for a surprise, but it's okay. Here's the thing: Connecting these dots isn't just some spiritual scavenger hunt. It's an absolute must for your growth and expansion. Once you start seeing these connections, everything that comes into your awareness gets filtered through an entirely new lens, much like going from standard definition to spiritual 4K Ultra HD. That's kinda the whole point.

Yeah, so maybe you find out that the "spiritual" stuff you used to think was whacked, crazy, or weird actually resonates within the deepest part of who *you* are. Maybe you realize you've been living someone else's definition of success. It's scary as hell because you might not like everything you uncover. But it's also the most honest, the most real, you've ever been with yourself, and there's something amazing about that. You start making decisions based on what actually "feels" right to you instead of what you think you're supposed to do.

That's right, I said "feels" right. When you peel everything back to the raw, authentic you, your entire being will feel it when something is right for you. Hold on a minute ... I don't know why, but the movie *Shrek* just popped into my head. You know, the scene where Shrek is talking about people/ogres having layers, and you peel back the layers like that of an onion. Donkey says something to the effect of, "You know what else has layers? Parfaits! Parfaits have layers, and everyone loves parfaits!" Do we need to take a snack break or should we push on? Okay, let's keep it going. Another exercise some people do is this thing called body testing. Body testing can be done by asking yes-or-no questions, and your body will either remain still, fall forward, or fall backward. It's really kind of cool. Learning to trust my body's wisdom was a game-changer. For someone who'd lived almost entirely in his head for decades, discovering that my body had intelligence and could communicate with me was revolutionary. It was like finding out I'd been carrying around a sophisticated guidance system my entire life without knowing how to use it. I do know some people who use body testing regularly; I, on the other hand, get a feeling in my gut and in my chest. No, it's not a heart attack or anything like that; my stomach starts to get butterflies, kind of like when you get nervous, and my chest starts to feel heavy, like when your chest is congested.

The interesting thing is that the more you connect with who you truly are, the authentic you, the more you start to understand why certain things have happened in your life, why you've been drawn to specific experiences or people, and why some people and situations have appeared when they did.

It's like the movie of your life starts making sense, but you're viewing it from a completely different lens. You begin to see patterns and connections that were invisible to you before, like your soul has been trying to steer you toward something all along, but you were always too busy following the compass of societal expectations to pay enough attention to the signs and your own internal compass. This shift in perspective was profound—from seeing my life as a series of random events that happened to me to recognizing it as a carefully orchestrated journey toward awakening. Even the painful experiences began to make sense as necessary catalysts for growth and self-discovery. And this new understanding would be essential as I moved into the next phase of my journey—the healing that had to happen once I'd uncovered all those buried wounds.

Spiritual Summary

Questioning everything you've ever believed in isn't a crisis—it's a freaking breakthrough, a gift. When you start pulling apart the labyrinth of conditioning that's been handed down through generations, you're not losing your mind; you're finally finding your soul. The uncomfortable awakening to how much of your life has been lived according to other people's rules and expectations is precisely what needs to happen before you can discover who you truly are beneath all those masks. Trust the process, even when it feels like everything is falling apart, because sometimes things need to fall apart before they can fall into place.

"Hurts So Good":
The Healing and Integration Stages

The transition from questioning everything to actively healing the wounds that questioning revealed was like moving from diagnosis to treatment. Once I could see all the places where I'd been carrying pain, limiting beliefs, and generational conditioning, the real work began—the work of healing those wounded parts of myself and integrating the insights into a new way of being. And let me tell you, this part of the journey wasn't just challenging—it was the spiritual equivalent of open-heart surgery without anesthesia.

John Cougar Mellencamp had it right with "Hurts So Good," especially how it begins. The lyrics discuss a young John Cougar-Mellencamp transitioning from his childhood ways and deciding it was time to start adulting. John does a masterful job of setting the stage for how we all start becoming who we're going to become. Our childhoods set the stage for our belief systems and the trajectory of most of our lives. Growing up in the 1970s and 1980s was vastly different from today, not just in terms of technology and modern conveniences, but in ways that extend far beyond those things and into the very essence of who we are as individuals and a society. This was a time when, let's say, if I were crying, my dad would give me the old "Stop crying, or I'll give you something to cry about" line. My dad wasn't terrible; I think he was just a product of the time. These types of responses were undoubtedly a root cause for many of us not dealing with emotions or challenges in a healthy way, and for us ignoring or burying them deep down inside, or what I like to call the "ostrich approach," only to have them rear their ugly heads for decades to come.

The realization that my childhood coping mechanisms had become adult survival strategies was both painful and liberating. The emotional suppression that had protected me as a child was now suffocating me as an adult, and it was time to learn new ways of being with difficult emotions.

In the healing stage of the twelve stages of spiritual awakening, as described by Dolores Cannon, the process of deep emotional, mental, spiritual, and sometimes even physical healing begins. As you've uncovered more about your true self and the hidden patterns buried deep down inside your life, this phase allows you to confront your old wounds, limiting beliefs, and unresolved emotions that no longer serve you. It's a process of letting go of the past and stepping into a lighter, more aligned version of yourself. I came to realize that healing is an active process, not a passive one. It actually requires some big-time effort on your part to begin the healing process. This was a crucial understanding for me—healing wasn't something that would happen to me, it was something I had to participate in fully and consciously. During the healing stage, things may bubble up that you haven't given much thought to in your life, as you may have been focused on simply surviving your situation rather than thriving in it. These could be abandonment issues, abuse issues, things you had no idea you were carrying with you from this lifetime or, as some find out, from several lifetimes, lifetimes you have now been tasked to remember and heal. By bringing these long-forgotten experiences to the surface, you can release emotional burdens and break free from patterns of fear, guilt, or pain. Ms. Cannon believed that by understanding and releasing past-life trauma, you can heal not only this lifetime but also the spiritual energy that you carry forward.

For me, there were many layers of healing to dig through. Let me take you back to second grade, when I was a latchkey kid before anyone thought to slap a super cool label on it. Like most kids in my neighborhood, I rode the bus to and from school—nothing revolutionary there, right? Except my daily commute was less "The Wheels on the Bus" and more *Lord of the Flies* meets *The Hunger Games*, minus the fantastic soundtrack, the sponsors, and fancy arena. We've already established that I was, shall we say, husky. Okay, fat. I was a tall, fat kid, which apparently, in the twisted logic of elementary school bullies, translates to "must destroy." Don't ask me to explain the psychology—it took me a long time to unpack that particular trauma carry-on bag with my therapist. But for whatever reason, I became the daily special on the bully menu: punch, kick, or trip the fat kid, with a side of emotional scarring. My parents weren't there to greet me with milk and cookies when I got home. They were working, or avoiding each other, or doing whatever people did in the '70s when their marriages were falling apart. No parenting guidebooks, no Instagram influencers telling them about "gentle parenting," no cell phones to coordinate who'd be home when. They played a daily game of marital chicken, both trying to come home when the other wouldn't be there, and both often losing.

Which meant—you guessed it—yours truly was *Home Alone* before Macaulay Culkin made it look fun.

Every. Single. Day. Same routine. As I'd walk down that narrow bus aisle toward my daily freedom, I'd get punched, kicked, or tripped before I could reach the door. It was like running a gauntlet, except instead of warriors with weapons, it was snot-nosed kids with their own anger issues. This particular day my exit started no differently, with one exception that would change everything. There were these two brothers—let's call them John and Erik (because those were their actual names and they're probably in prison now).

These intellectual giants took particular joy in making my 150-foot journey from the bus stop to my front door feel like crossing the beaches of Normandy. One hundred and fifty feet. That's it. That's like, what, half a football field? Should take thirty seconds, tops. But imagine having to fight your way through every single foot of it while two future felons used you as a punching bag, all while you're screaming, "Mom, can you come help me?" to a house you know is empty. At least these criminal masterminds weren't bright enough to realize Mom wasn't home. Small victories, right? Remember, I said there was an exception this day? Well, buckle up, baby. I'd been programmed like a good little victim: Don't fight back. Fighting was bad. Fighting got you sent to the principal's office. Fighting got you in trouble at home which made school punishment look like a vacation. So, I took it. Day after day, I took it. But this day, as I reached the bottom step of the bus, there they were—the brothers grim, rubbing their hands together like cartoon villains, discussing what they were going to do to me. Out loud. Like I was a science project in "How to Traumatize a Fat Kid 101." John pushed. Erik crouched behind me—the classic bully move, sophisticated as a whoopee cushion. John pushed again. I went down like a sack of husky Russet potatoes. They laughed their stupid, sinister laughs. Picture a turtle on its back. Got it? Now make that turtle chubby and crying. That was me, scrambling to get up while they stood over me, laughing. But then—and this is where the universe threw me a bone—I saw it. My lunch box, on its side, gleaming in the afternoon sun like Excalibur waiting to be pulled from the stone. In the 1970s, our lunch boxes were made of metal. Real, skull-cracking metal. Mine was an Evel Knievel lunch box, because apparently even my lunch storage needed to be ironic—here I was, barely able to walk home without getting destroyed, carrying a lunch box featuring a guy who literally got famous for surviving spectacular crashes.

Something inside of me snapped. Or maybe something in me finally woke up. Instead of my usual grab-and-run technique, I grabbed that lunch box and became the fucking lunch box vigilante, like Thor swinging his magnificent hammer, Mjölnir. *Wham!* Right across the back of Erik's head while he was still on the ground, laughing. The sound was beautiful—like freaking justice wrapped in metal with Evel Knievel's smiling face on it. John stood there stunned, his puny bully brain unable to process that the victim had become the victor. That's when I swung that lunch box across his face like I was freaking Babe Ruth calling his shot. Not once, but twice. Because if you're going to snap, you might as well make it count, right? The handle broke on the second swing, sending my beloved Evel Knievel lunch box spinning off into the suburban wilderness. And that's when I ran. I ran like my life depended on it—because honestly, it probably did. These kids didn't grow up to be youth pastors, if you know what I mean. Thank God we didn't lock doors in the '70s (different times, guys). I burst through that front door, slammed it shut, locked it, and slid down to the floor like I was in some horror movie, except instead of looking cool, I was a terrified second grader having a complete breakdown. First came the laughter—holy shit, I'd actually fought back! Then came their pounding on the door, screaming they were going to kill me (a couple of real charmers, these two). That's when the laughter turned to tears—uncontrollable, snot-bubble-producing, body-shaking sobs. I sat there on that tiny, tiled foyer floor, alone and terrified, until they finally got bored and left.

When my mom eventually came home, the house was still dark. She found me there, curled up on the floor of our tiny foyer, probably looking like the world's saddest welcome mat. I told her everything. And for once—maybe the only time I can remember—she went full Mama Bear. The next day, she drove me to school and had what I can only assume was a "come to Jesus" meeting with the principal and my teacher, Mrs. Wiley. Whatever she said must have been Goddamn epic, because from that day forward, Mr. Fish, our bus driver (yes, that was his real name, and yes, it's perfect), made sure I was dropped off directly at my driveway, while the other kids, including the Bully Brothers, were dropped off a few hundred yards away at their new stop. Mr. Fish became my yellow bus guardian angel. He made damn sure nothing like that ever happened to me again. Sometimes heroes wear capes. Sometimes they wear trucker caps and drive school buses. That broken Evel Knievel lunch box was a lifesaver that day, or at least it became a lifeline—or at least my little metal connection to sanity. Either way, somewhere out there in the universe, Evel Knievel owes me a new lunch box. And John and Erik? They did spend some time in the penal system, which is too bad, I suppose. Some may feel they may owe me something, but I'll settle for knowing I was the fat kid who fought back that one day.

This healing process is holistic, touching every aspect of who you are—physically, emotionally, mentally, and spiritually. As you begin to clear away old wounds and baggage, you create space—a new space—for a higher level of consciousness and a more peaceful, happy life. In my case, this was true on all accounts. For most of my life, with very few exceptions, I had dealt with being overweight. Hell, I will go so far as to say, according to my medical files, "morbidly obese." I guess Bon Jovi's "Wanted Dead or Alive" might have been a good choice for the musical accompaniment, too.

"Wanted Dead or Alive"
Bon Jovi

When I began my unwitting journey of spiritual awakening, I was nearly four hundred pounds of rumbling, stumbling pain. I was in emotional pain, physical pain, and certainly, spiritual pain. I realize there are classifications for types of pain, but ultimately, pain is pain. The weight wasn't just physical—it was the accumulated mass of every emotion I'd stuffed down, every dream I'd abandoned, every authentic part of myself I'd buried under layers of protection.

Spiritual Summary

Healing isn't something that happens to you while you sit around waiting; it's active work. Think of it as spiritual open-heart surgery without anesthesia, and you have to show up and participate. All that shit you buried as a kid because you were too busy surviving to deal with it—it's still in there, and at some point, you're going to have to dig through every painful layer of it if you want to stop carrying it around like a trauma carry-on bag. The good news is that when you finally clear out the old wounds and limiting beliefs, you make space for something better. As in a lighter, more aligned version of yourself who no longer needs a metal lunch box to feel powerful any longer. Sometimes fighting back, even just once, changes everything, and the healing that follows changes even more than you can imagine.

The Quantum Timeline Theory:
Healing Across Time and Space

Now, this is where the healing journey took a turn I never saw coming. I won't bore you all with a description of the multiverse and quantum timelines; hell, maybe I will, a little bit of woo-woo won't hurt you, because this shit is wild when you really think about it. The basic idea is that there are infinite versions of reality happening simultaneously, like infinite TV channels all playing different versions of your life at the same time. In some realities, you made other choices, had different experiences, or even lived in entirely different times altogether. The quantum timeline theory suggests that all moments—past, present, and future—are happening simultaneously. Time isn't the straight line we think it is; it's more like a big ball of squiggly, tangled stuff, like a ball of yarn. That ball of yarn can be one string; you're the string in this example. So when you're doing healing work, you're not just revisiting memories—you're actually connecting with other versions of yourself that exist in these parallel timelines. *Kaboom!*, mind blown, and now drop the mic. Now, I know how absolutely, 100 percent batshit crazy this sounds. Trust me, the rational part of my brain is still screaming, "What the hell are you talking about, dude?" But here's the thing—when you're in these deep meditative states or regression sessions, it doesn't feel like you're remembering something that happened.

It feels like you're there, interacting with that younger version of yourself who exists in real time, or observing it, like you're watching television, just in a different dimension or timeline.

Kelly would guide me into these states where I could go back and provide comfort, wisdom, and healing to past versions of myself who were stuck in trauma. It's like being able to time-travel, but instead of changing history, you're healing it. The idea is that when you heal those wounded aspects of yourself across different timelines, it creates a ripple effect that improves your current reality. I realize that what I'm saying sounds far-fetched; believe me, I still struggle to wrap my mind around it. There have been too many occasions when these things have stepped in at the right time to help talk me off the ledge and, more importantly, helped light a path for me to walk down and begin to heal. Whether it's actual quantum physics or just an effective therapeutic technique that my brain thinks is real, I honestly don't give a shit anymore. What matters is that it works. The pragmatic approach I eventually adopted served me well—if something consistently produces positive results in my life, I don't need to understand the mechanism completely to benefit from it. The proof is in the healing, not in the theory. Healing is a constant process; some things still find their way into my life to cause me pain, but I know that I'm good and I'm on the right path, and the proof is staring at me in the mirror each time I look into it.

Spiritual Summary

Time isn't a straight line; it's more like a tangled ball of yarn, and you're the string running through it, which means healing isn't just about revisiting memories—it's about connecting with versions of yourself who are still stuck in trauma across different timelines. I know how crazy that sounds, and honestly, the rational part of my brain still screams, "What the hell?" every time I think about it. But here's what I've learned: If something consistently heals you and improves your life, you don't need to understand the quantum physics behind it. The proof is in the healing, not the theory. Whether it's actual science or just an effective technique that my brain thinks is real, I honestly don't give a shit anymore, because it works.

A Powerful Healing Session with Kelly

One particular healing session with Kelly Schwegel stands out as a defining moment in my healing journey. During a class, she asked me a direct question that left me stumped. She hadn't asked me to solve a scientific equation or anything; she simply asked me what happened to me between the ages of nine and ten. For the life of me, I couldn't give her an answer. The fact that I had such a complete blank spot in my memory should have been a red flag, but I hadn't recognized the significance of missing memories until that moment. She was patient with me for a while, and then Kelly suggested that we try meditation, if I was willing to give it a go. Since meditation was something new for me, I was all for it, and so it began. The meditation Kelly was guiding me through was called "Healing the Younger Yous." Kelly proceeded to bring me back to when I was nine years old. What was slightly unnerving later was that it seemed as though Kelly was viewing what was going on in my head, as if it were on a movie screen that she could see too. She could see me standing at the end of the driveway, waving goodbye to my mom as she left to go out of town. She then saw me in the classroom when I was in third grade and heard and observed what my third-grade teacher was saying and doing to me, which, by today's standards, would have had her run out of town. The vivid nature of these recovered memories was startling. They weren't vague impressions or fragmented images—they were complete, detailed scenes playing out with full sensory experiences. And Kelly's ability to witness them as they unfolded in my consciousness was both comforting and slightly creepy.

Kelly's voice was cracking as she continued to guide me through the meditation, and she apologized for the discomfort I was experiencing. She continued to support me emotionally and spiritually, encouraging me to keep going and, all the while, assuring me that things would be resolved once we finished the meditation.

Kelly said that she could see me, alone in the hallway, left there to understand why I was out in the hall in the first place, and why I wasn't allowed back in the classroom with the other students. Kelly asked if I could see myself sitting at the desk, in the hallway, alone. I could in fact see myself, staring at the dark wooden desk, my head down, and upset.

The image of that nine-year-old boy, isolated and ashamed, broke my heart. He looked so innocent and confused, trying to understand what he had done wrong, carrying the weight of adult disapproval that was too much for him to process at his/my young age. She then asked me if I would like to say anything to my nine-year-old self, if I had the opportunity, and I immediately said, "Yes, of course." She encouraged me to go up to the younger me and say what was in my heart.

I slowly walked up to the younger version of myself. As I came closer to this younger version of me, I was trembling inside; I had a flurry of emotions that ran the gambit from sorrow to being so angry that this was happening to a child, to me! As I reached my place next to the younger version of me, a quiet calm fell over me, a warmth that caused all of the other emotions I had been feeling up to this point to dissipate. What I was feeling now was the only thing that truly matters in our lives, and that was love and compassion. Love for the little boy who was missing this very thing in his life. Compassion for a child who was being judged and left alone to figure out what he had done to deserve this banishment. Of course he felt alone, with no support and no one to tell him he wasn't bad; he was a young boy starving for attention in any way he could find it. As I knelt down, I began to comfort the nine-year-old version of me.

"Hey, pal, can we talk? I'd like you to know something. I want you to know that you aren't a bad person. You also have no reason to feel ashamed of yourself. You, my man, are a gift. You are a bright, shining light that grows into an incredibly kind and compassionate man. You become so strong and confident in who you truly are, that these situations no longer happen. As a matter of fact, you grow into the kind of person who is a wonderful example of how to treat people. You are an example to many people, especially the three boys that you have the privilege of calling your sons. I need you to believe this next part . . . I am here with you now, and I will *always* be here for you and remind you of who you really are. You believe me when I say that, right?" *Mmm hmm.* "One more thing, I want to let you know that you are loved, you *are* love."

Kelly reiterated this to me in her emotionally shaky voice as well. She quietly told me, in a quivering whisper, "You are loved. You are worthy of love, support, and all the blessings the universe has in store for you." This exchange between my adult self and my younger self was profoundly healing in ways I couldn't have anticipated. It was like being both the loving parent and the hurt child simultaneously, providing myself with the comfort and validation I'd needed for decades, and never realized until that moment.

Kelly gently let me know that the time with the younger version of me was coming to an end, but I could always go back to provide support, love, and guidance to that version or any other version of myself that needed a little help getting unstuck. When I opened my eyes, there was Kelly, with tears rolling down her face, which showed up even on our Zoom call. It's as if she were experiencing the same pain as I was—she wasn't abandoning me, leaving me to figure it all out alone. Kelly was my spiritual sherpa, my sacred companion who offered up her heart to help me heal. Why risk all this suffering when it's not her problem? This is when you know you've met a true healer—a guardian angel who happens to live here on Earth, in Wisconsin, to be completely honest. She let me know that this was what she had been referring to earlier, the pain that needed healing, but for many reasons, I hadn't recalled any of it before the meditation. Maybe the more honest answer is, I didn't want to remember it any longer. The protective amnesia that had shielded me from traumatic memories as a child was no longer serving me as an adult—it was time to remember, process the emotions, and to finally heal.

Spiritual Summary

Sometimes the most powerful healing happens when you go back and become the loving adult that your wounded child self desperately needed but never had. That nine-year-old version of you who was left alone, ashamed, and starving for attention. He or she's still in there, waiting for someone to kneel down and tell them they're not bad, they aren't broken, and they're worthy of love. And when a true healer shows up, someone willing to walk through your pain alongside you with tears rolling down her own face, you know you've found an earthly guardian angel, not someone who's going to leave you alone to figure it all out by yourself. The protective amnesia that shielded you as a child isn't serving you anymore; it's time to remember, process, and finally let that wounded part of you know that everything turned out okay.

Integration: Bringing Healing into Daily Life

The healing work I'd done with Kelly was profound, but healing in a meditation session is one thing—integrating that healing into your daily life is a whole other beast. I also sought out a therapist, which Kelly suggested I do, as therapists can be particularly beneficial when used in conjunction with other healing modalities. Being able to discuss deeply personal experiences with someone who comes from a judgment-free zone is freeing, to put it mildly. This holistic approach, where I brought in a spiritual mentor, a mental health professional, and a heavy reliance on a willingness to expand and be open to new things and new ways of thinking, was a huge part in shedding the me that no longer served my highest good, and helped give birth to the version of me that was healthy, kind, and open to ways of thinking and living that now are a part of my life. The idea that your body, mind, and spirit all work together to form you is not bullshit, like I might have once thought, but it's exactly as advertised. When one of these things is out of balance, the others quickly become unbalanced and require your attention and effort. My healing journey had begun, and I was energized by everything I was learning.

What's interesting about this time was that people I hadn't seen in a while would tell me there was something different about me, but they couldn't put their finger on it. Well ... I'm sure it didn't hurt that I had quite literally gotten rid of the old me, or at least one hundred and fifty pounds of the old me; that could be one thing that was different about me. However, the change went far deeper than physical transformation. There was something different in my energy, my presence, the way I carried myself through the world. The shame and self-hatred that had weighed me down for decades were now lifting, replaced by something lighter, more authentic, more alive. Was it a coincidence that I went through this metamorphosis? I don't think so; I don't believe that the person I was becoming was a coincidence or an accident. This was the version of the person I had always been, but for years, I tried to hide from it through an abundance of weight. I had, metaphorically of course, done away with the old me and birthed a new me that felt comfortable in his own skin, and wasn't ashamed to let people know how it all came about.

Kelly Schwegel was the first person to shed light on my spiritual path, which opened the door to others, and for that, I am forever grateful. The Les Brown quote comes to mind as we segue into the interconnected stage of integration: "To achieve something you've never achieved before, you must become someone you've never been before." That pretty much sums it up. How does this change stick around for a while? Well, it's by introducing it into all facets of your life that you reach the integration stage. The integration stage is a pivotal point in the twelve stages of spiritual awakening journeys, as described by Dolores Cannon. It's where all the insights and truths you've uncovered in earlier stages come together, and you begin aligning your life with this new awareness. It's one thing to realize your spiritual nature, but it's another to fully live it. In this phase, spiritual understanding blends seamlessly into your everyday experiences, guiding your thoughts, actions, and decisions. At this stage of awakening, you start to see how the lessons you've learned—whether they involve self-awareness, healing, or past-life connections—apply to your real-world interactions. Ms. Cannon's teachings emphasize that true spiritual growth isn't just about the inner work; it's about integrating that knowledge into how you live your life. You might notice yourself making subtle yet powerful changes, such as releasing toxic habits and yes, even toxic people, adopting new practices that nurture and nourish your soul, or setting boundaries that honor your growth and keep the garbage out.

This stage of the spiritual awakening process involves a deep acceptance of the truths you've discovered and the responsibility to align your actions with this new/old higher consciousness. Integration means living in harmony with your soul's purpose, allowing your spiritual journey to guide you through day-to-day life in a more meaningful and connected way.

Spiritual Summary

Healing in a meditation session is one thing, but integrating that healing into your actual life is a whole other beast, and that's where the real transformation happens. Turns out the idea that your body, mind, and spirit all work together isn't bullshit like I once thought; when one is out of whack, the others follow, and getting them aligned is what finally let me shed a hundred and fifty pounds of weight and decades of shame I'd been hiding behind. To become someone you've never been, you have to be willing to release the toxic habits, the toxic people, and the old version of yourself that no longer serves you, and then actually live your spiritual understanding, not just talk about it. Integration means your spiritual growth stops being something you do and starts being who you are.

Exploring Different Healing Modalities

As my integration deepened, I discovered that healing comes in many forms, and different approaches work for different people. There are several forms of healing and healers that fall within the spiritual walls we're discussing.

Dr. Julie Foster is a gifted energy healer who uses craniosacral healing as one of her many healing modalities. Dr. Foster also utilizes medical acupuncture in her practice, complemented by Western medical techniques that create a holistic approach to the healing process for her patients.

Kerry Müller employs a variety of modalities in her healing practice as well. Kerry is an RTT clinical hypnotherapist, a certified crystal healer, a certified chakra healer, a breath coach, and a certified sound therapist, one of my personal favorites. The science behind frequency and therapeutic applications has become increasingly popular, even in Western medicine. Some scientists have studied what happens when you expose the human body to sound vibrations—not just any sound, but the really low, rumbly stuff you feel in your chest more than you hear with your ears. They found that vibrations can stimulate blood vessel cells, activate nerve-calming proteins, and even help muscles and bones repair themselves. Kerry actually uses a machine called a Rife machine, which targets particular parts of the body with precise frequencies to facilitate cellular healing.

There's also a therapy that Julie Grant uses in her spiritual practice, called family constellation therapy. Julie Grant is a member of Jen Weigel's Spiritual Social Club (which is how I met this magnificent soul), and is a highly talented and kind healer. For those of you who haven't heard of this practice, Bert Hellinger was the originator of this work, which has evolved dramatically since its inception. The ultimate goal is to allow freedom to emerge. Julie's practice takes it a step further. Hell, Julie's practice takes it a few thousand steps further and includes some quantum leaps along the way, too. In her sessions, Julie helps heal generational trauma. What is generational trauma? Think of it this way: Generational trauma is an energetic blockage that we carry in our bodies from our ancestors. It can affect relationships, work, money, and our health, for starters. Another way to put it, at least in terms that I can relate to, is that your family's dysfunction doesn't just disappear when you grow up—it gets passed down like some twisted, crappy inheritance nobody wants. Julie works with you to help unravel and release the blocks that are present in your life, which is freaking awesome! Man, I wish I had known Julie Grant years ago; it would have saved me thousands of dollars and hundreds of hours that I spent in a therapist's office. Nothing wrong with seeing a therapist, mind you. I see a therapist, and I'm all right, hahaha! At least that's what I tell myself, but the verdict may still be out on that with some of you.

What can you expect from a session with Julie? Speaking from my perspective and my session with Julie, I can say that I found it extremely helpful and it opened my eyes to some things I hadn't even considered before. The focus is on dealing with generational trauma, recognizing unhealthy family patterns, and processing grief and unresolved emotions—especially around family members who've passed away. The session was kind of magical, really. It cleared away some emotional clusterfucks that seemed to repeat through my life. Just make sure you're in a good headspace before diving into a session. Julie does a remarkable job ensuring that you're comfortable, feel safe, and are confident about doing the work. This is certainly one way to heal some of your family traumas and might just have you feeling a little lighter once it's over. At least that's how I felt; I was no longer playing the part of good old Jacob Marley from *Scrooge*. I wonder if Jacob was related to Bob Marley? Hmm . . . Buffalo Soldier, stop it!

"Buffalo Soldier"
Bob Marley

In all seriousness, the exploration of these different healing modalities taught me that there's no one right way to heal. Each approach offers something unique, and often it's the combination of multiple approaches that creates the most profound transformation. The key is staying open to what calls to you, even if—especially if—it sounds a little weird at first.

Spiritual Summary

Healing the wounded parts of yourself—especially the scared, hurt kid inside—isn't just spiritual work, it's some of the most important freaking work you'll ever do. Whether it's through meditation, therapy, or revisiting the pain of your younger self, the healing process requires you to become both the wounded child and the loving adult who can finally provide what was missing. Integration means taking all that inner healing work and living it in your daily life, not just talking about it. When you heal your past pain and integrate your spiritual growth, you can become a different person—and I guarantee that everyone around you will notice, even if they can't put their finger on what's changed. It isn't a what in this case, it's a who. The real magic happens when healing becomes not something you do, but something you are—an ongoing process of becoming more whole, more authentic, more you.

"Blowin' in the Wind":
When Intuition Becomes Prophecy

Bob Dylan wrote about questions without easy answers, suggesting that sometimes the truth is as elusive and untouchable as the wind itself—always present, but impossible to hold in your hands.

"Blowin' in the Wind"
Bob Dylan

That's exactly how I felt about what happened next. The wind carries things we can't see, whispers we can't quite hear, and sometimes, just sometimes, it brings us knowledge we're not supposed to have yet. The transition from healing my own wounds to experiencing prophetic knowing happened gradually at first, then all at once. Initially, the "prophetic knowing" would be presented in my dreams. These weren't ordinary dreams, mind you; these dreams were so lucid and real that even after waking up from a sound sleep, I wasn't sure if what I was recalling had really happened or not. The transition, as I mentioned, wasn't immediate; however, after some time, what I once had to fall asleep to feel was now happening with my eyes open, and oftentimes, it was presented as if the situation had already occurred. It was a recollection, a knowing of an outcome. I didn't have a clue as to why I knew . . . or how I knew . . . but I did. This is referred to as claircognizance. Claircognizance is basically the psychic ability of "just knowing shit" without any logical explanation—like when your brain suddenly downloads information from the cosmic Wi-Fi without you even knowing the password. It's that moment when you absolutely *know* something is true even though you have zero evidence, no one told you, and you didn't Google That Shit; the answer just appears in your head like a spiritual pop-up ad you actually wanted. This might show up as random "aha!" moments where solutions to problems just materialize while you're scrub-a-dub-dubbing in the shower, or those gut feelings about people that turn out to be spot-on even though you can't explain why Peter from accounting gives you weird vibes. (Spoiler: He's probably the one stealing your coworkers' lunches.) Some people get sudden flashes of insight during the most mundane moments—driving, washing dishes, pretending to work—and boom, they suddenly know exactly what to do about that situation they weren't even thinking about. The really gifted claircognizant folks can give advice about stuff they've never experienced, make decisions without making pro/con lists, and basically function like human Magic 8 Balls, except you won't get the Try Again Later message; their answers actually make sense. Bottom line: Claircognizance is when your inner knowing bypasses your logical brain entirely and just drops truth bombs directly into your consciousness, no assembly required.

More often than not, our spiritual gifts, like claircognizance, don't announce themselves with fanfare, rather they slip into our consciousness quietly, like old friends we've always known but never properly met. Hey, by the way . . . every human on this planet has access to spiritual gifts. Yeah, even your weird neighbor who collects cement geese statues, with all the different outfits to match the changing seasons. In retrospect, I guess the geese beat the hell out of the old lawn jockeys that used to adorn people's front porch steps.

It's actually our natural state to be connected to all things, but here's the ethereal joke: We enter this world at birth with our hard drives completely wiped clean, forgetting where we came from and how we ended up here. It's exactly like when Will Smith waves his neuralyzer wand in *Men in Black*—FLASH!—and suddenly you can't remember shit about being an infinite spiritual being. What we're doing with all this awakening stuff is what I like to call "re-remembering" who we are—literally putting chunks of us back together, bringing back parts of ourselves that have been scattered like puzzle pieces in a tornado. Or like when you drop a jigsaw puzzle and your dog decides those pieces need to be in seven different rooms. That's spiritual awakening, folks—finding your pieces and remembering you came with the complete set all along.

This next experience showed me that the sensitivity I'd been trying to suppress my whole life was actually a direct line to information I couldn't possibly know through normal channels. Some people may consider this to be stage three, stage four, or stage five in their spiritual journey of awakening. I don't know exactly what stage it was for me, but there was definitely something happening. The boundaries between intuition and prophecy were beginning to blur, and I was about to discover that sometimes we know things not because we're psychic, but because on some level, we're all connected to a universal consciousness that transcends time and space.

Here's where there are more questions than answers, at least for me. Remember, in my household growing up, this sort of "spiritual, woo-woo shit" would never have been accepted in a million years. My dad was a Mason, which is founded in religion. My mom was in the Eastern Star, which was the coed version of the Masonic Rite, and for a number of years she followed suit with the religious rules in the house. To further explain, my dad was the kind of guy who attended church every Sunday, served as an usher during the services, and volunteered for any and every church activity he could. The church and the parish were very important to him, and became his extended family. Had I approached my father with the "I see dead people" line from *The Sixth Sense*, I would have been smacked across the head all the way to the church, up the steps, and it would have continued until I was seated in the front row. That kind of "crap" didn't fly with him. I'm confident my dad would have found this sort of lifestyle embarrassing in comparison to the well-defined, color-within-the-lines, stay-inside-of-your-box church belief system. I will say my dad became a little more understanding and tolerant later in his life. I mean a little, as in very little, but at least it was something. The fact that he softened even slightly gave me hope that maybe, just maybe, these experiences weren't as crazy as I'd been taught to believe.

Looking back, I'd like to share something remarkable that happened on April 11, 1994. If you're anything like me, you probably go to the store for milk and come home with cereal, bananas, and paper towels, but no milk. Raise your hand if that's ever happened to you. I'd need about ten more hands to be even semi-accurate in my account of absent-mindedness. However, this experience is forever etched in my brain with a clarity that defies my usual scattered attention. April 11, 1994, was a Monday, and I worked for a waterbed retailer in the Chicagoland area. A coworker of mine was notorious for making excuses to leave early, and I don't recall his particular reason that day. But he was out of the store by 5:00 p.m., like clockwork. It had been slow most of the day until around 6:30

that night, when it felt like a tour bus opened its doors, right in front of the store, and everyone on the tour wanted to buy a waterbed or furniture. The phone rang as I was chatting with a couple, trying to help them find the type of bed they were looking for.

I looked at the couple and said, "Mmm . . . that's my mom calling."

"Oh, was she supposed to be calling you now?" the wife asked.

"Nope, I just know it's her."

The knowingness was absolute. I was so sure that I didn't question it for a second. It was the same kind of knowing I'd experienced as a four-year-old being called to my closet, but now, decades later, I was beginning to understand that these moments of knowing weren't random—they were spiritual gifts trying to prepare me for what was coming. As people kept piling in, the doorbell kept dinging away, as if it were mocking me and telling me to get a move on.

"Thank you for calling H_2O Kingdom; this is Jim. How may I help you?"

I made sure to say it loud enough for everyone in the showroom to hear, "Oh, hi, Mom!" I looked over and smiled at the couple. They and everyone within earshot got a chuckle from that.

"Hi, baby, are you busy?"

"Yep, I'm slammed, Mom. I have twelve customers in the store, and it's just me."

"Oh, Bill left early again?"

"Yeah, he left early . . . again."

"Well then, I won't keep you. I love you, and I'll see you later."

"I love you too, Mom, and I'll see ya later."

I hung up, went back to the customers, and carried on. I did my best to catch up, but there were still six patient customers when the phone rang again about an hour and a half later.

"Thank you for calling H$_2$O Kingdom; this is Jim. How may I help you?"

"Jim?"

"Yes, this is Jim."

"Hi, Jim, this is Pat, your mom's friend from the hospital."

My mom was an RN and the head nurse of two emergency rooms, as well as the head nurse of the county correctional facility's medical department. She was quite possibly the hardest-working person I have ever met.

"Jim, your mom was in an accident. It's okay, but we need you to get here as soon as you can."

"Accident?! Is she okay?"

"Take your time; it's not a big rush. Just get here."

Pat hung up the phone. I spun around and announced to all the remaining customers in the showroom that I had to close the store due to an emergency, and apologized. I quickly called the corporate office to let them know what was happening. I tried counting the drawer for the day so as not to leave that for anyone else, but all the while, I kept hearing a voice saying, *Just leave it. Let's go!* I decided to listen to that voice and locked the door, then ran to the fuse box where we turned off all the lights in the showroom, and raced back to the front, only to see a dude with his hands cupped against the glass peering longingly at our waterbed conditioner display. That's the thing about waterbeds—you needed to put conditioner in yearly, otherwise it would smell like you were sleeping in a swamp. I unlocked the door to leave, and the guy tried to push his way in, saying he came all the way down here to buy conditioner and . . . and . . . I cut him off.

"Hey, pal, I'm really sorry, but there was an emergency, and I need to leave, like right now."

"Well, this is an emergency too, and I did drive all the way down here for this stuff."

My head was about to pop off with this motherfucker, but I refrained and said, "Okay, hang on." I ran back inside, grabbed the conditioner, and tossed it to him. "Happy Birthday."

"Hey, it was my birthday yesterday, but thanks." The dude stood there, as if he wanted to carry on a conversation with me.

"I gotta go. Sorry!"

I pulled out of the parking lot, and the guy just stood there, looking like I hurt his feelings. Maybe I did, I'm not sure. As I started driving to the hospital, twenty-five minutes away from the showroom, a voice in my head said, *"Mom's dead."*

"Stop it! Mom's not dead!"

"Yes, she is, Mom's dead."

I knew she was dead, but dammit, I didn't want to have to come to grips with that. I began tearing up as the possibility of this being real came crashing down.

I called Pat at the hospital from my big-ass brick mobile phone with the big rubber antenna, which was totally cool back in the day. Pat came to the phone, and I cut to the chase and asked, "Is my mom dead, Pat?"

"How far away are you now, Jim?"

"I'm like ten minutes away."

"Okay, take your time, and we'll see you in a few minutes." Pat hung up.

"She's dead, dammit, I know she is . . . what the fuck is happening?!"

I called my fraternity brother, who's still one of my best friends to this day, Kevin.

"My mom was in an accident, and I think she's dead."

"What?! Slow down there, Sparky; what do you mean you think she's dead?"

"I know the lady my mom works with at the hospital, Pat, and she said she was in an accident, there's no rush, be careful, but get here as soon as you can."

"It sounds like everything is okay from what you're telling me."

"No, I'm telling you, I think my mom's *dead!*"

"Okay, which hospital are you going to, the one in Naperville or Joliet?"

"Joliet."

"Okay, I'll be there in an hour."

Understand this: Kevin lived at least an hour and a half away from the hospital where my mom worked. The man drove his car like he stole it sometimes, which I am thankful for: Kevin's lead foot. I drove toward the entrance of the emergency room and found a parking spot at the front of the lot. It was as if someone had saved it for me. I hauled ass through the automatic doors at the entrance, gave a quick wave to the security guard whom I had seen on several occasions, and made a beeline for the emergency room intake desk, where Pat was waiting to meet me.

She said, "Hi, Jim, follow me."

I thought, Oh, maybe I was wrong. Maybe my mom's already in a room, and she's fine after all.

We got to a room that reminded me of the practice studios at DePaul University, which were soundproof for all intents and purposes.

The door closed, and Pat turned and said, "Jim, I'm sorry to say that, yes, your mom's dead."

I'm sure it hurt Pat to say those words, nearly as much as it hurt me to hear them.

"How?" I whispered.

"She was in an accident involving multiple cars on Route 59, near Black Road. She died while she was in the ambulance. I'm sorry, but I need you to identify the body."

"Is she really banged up, Pat? I'm . . . I'm . . . not sure I—I can't, Pat. I can't see her like that. It's just . . . I can't do it," I muttered.

"We called your dad, too, so he should be here soon. It's okay, it can wait." And out the door she went.

I grabbed my phone and dialed my Aunt Shell, letting her know that she needed to use her three-way calling feature thingy and get Gram and Gramp on the phone right away, and that Mom had been in an accident. Seconds later, Aunt Shell, Gram, and Gramp were on the line.

"Okay, we're here."

"Mom was in a car accident earlier tonight, and she's dead."

I don't know why, but I just blurted it out. I guess I figured there was no time for small talk or subtleties in this instance; it just came out, and that's when I heard blood-curdling screams that sounded as though a soul was being brutally ripped apart, from both my grandmother and my Aunt Shell—that distinct wail of heartfelt loss and agony still echoes in the halls of my mind.

As I look back on it today, I notice that it was my intuition kicking in, telling me it was my mom who was calling during a rush at the waterbed store, and of course, the unbearable news that one of my closest friends and most trusted confidants, my mom, had passed away.

Spiritual Summary

Your intuition doesn't always speak in whispers—sometimes it screams at you through a knowing you can't explain. When that voice in your head tells you something that defies logic, pay attention. The same spiritual awareness that lets you know who's calling before you answer the phone can also prepare you for life's most devastating moments. This isn't a gift you ask for, but it's one that can help you navigate through the seemingly impossible. Trust that inner knowing, even when—especially when—you don't want it to be true. Sometimes the universe gives us these moments of preparation as an act of mercy, a way to begin processing what we're not ready to face.

"If Tomorrow Never Comes"

Garth Brooks wrote about the what-ifs in life, the regret of never telling someone how you truly felt about them. He sang about losing loved ones who never knew how much they were loved, living with the regret that true feelings were never revealed. That's exactly how I felt after losing my mom. The avalanche of emotions I felt that evening was surreal. I couldn't wrap my head around the fact that my mom was actually gone. I could no longer expect to receive those annoyingly cheery calls or impromptu visits at work or my house; they would never happen again, and I would never see her again. Before I left the hospital, Pat made sure to stop by the grieving room—which is what I later found was the official name of the room I was in—to make sure I was okay to drive home. I assured her that I would make it home safely and thanked her again for everything, as well as for checking on me. At this point, I'm sure my eyes looked as though I was pepper-sprayed by a fire hose; they felt like someone pepper-sprayed me, too. I held it together long enough to walk through the overflowing emergency room lobby and walk through the automated doors into the parking lot. I was no more than two steps from the sidewalk when I broke down again.

How did this happen? Why did it happen? This has got to be a bad dream I can't wake up from; it's just impossible. But it was not only possible; it had happened—my mom was gone.

I jumped in the car and started to make my way back home when my phone rang. It was my buddy, Kevin. I answered, and he was the one doing all of the talking for a change. Kevin had lost his dad years ago when he was only in eighth grade. The loss of a parent is something that is always with you at some point or another for the rest of your life. Kevin asked me at least a dozen times if I wanted him to come by and hang out. But it was pretty late at this point, and I just wanted to get home. I suggested he come by the next day if that was cool, and he, of course, said he'd be there and would call when he was on his way. Kevin is still one of those friends you can call any time of the day or night, and he will be there as quickly as possible. If you have one of those friends in your life, consider yourself lucky.

As I was pulling into my apartment complex, none of the lights that usually illuminated the path to my parking spot were lit. I honestly didn't care at this point; I was numb and pretty much unfazed by anything that was out of the norm, because nothing was normal now. I made it to the entryway, up the stairs, and into my apartment. As I walked numbly down the hallway, I didn't turn on a single light. I suppose, looking back, I wanted my surroundings to match my mood, which was dark and lifeless. Remember the avalanche of emotions I mentioned previously? Well, they landed on me as soon as I lay in bed. I didn't change my clothes—hell, I didn't even take my shoes off—I just collapsed into my bed and started feeling all the feels. I was riddled with guilt for all of the times I didn't tell my mom I loved her. I was ashamed of my pigheadedness of how long I held a grudge and didn't speak with her. I picked myself apart to the point I just kept saying, "I'm so sorry, Mom" over and over. I stopped my loop of "I'm sorrys" with a wish. I wished for what anyone would wish for in this situation—I wished for the opportunity to see her one last time, to tell her how I truly felt and how much she meant to me, but that wouldn't happen. At least that's what I thought at that time.

While I lay on my back and stared at the ceiling, I noticed a light coming through the bottom of the door. It was a soft, warm glow that might come from a holiday candle. That wouldn't have been a big deal if I had a roommate coming in from a late night out, but I didn't have a roommate. I also didn't leave a light on, because I never turned one on, nor was there a window that would allow for someone's headlights to peek through the doorway. This light had none of those origins. I had no idea why or how something like this could be happening. Here's the thing, though—I was just asking God to let me see my mom one more time, and in some way, I have to think that God heard my prayer because there was a light in the hallway, now growing more intense from under my door, inching its way inside the room. Was it her? Was the light in the hallway my mom? Was this what it felt like to have a psychotic episode? I'm asking for a friend. What in the hell was going on? To say I was a little scared would have been like saying the Titanic had a small leak. I was in the frozen state of fight, flight, or freeze; truly, I could not move. "I'm so sorry, Mom; I can't see you now. I'm so ashamed of myself. I love you; I'm sorry, but I just can't."

As quickly and strangely as the light appeared, the light vanished, and the familiar dark stillness of the night was back. I never spoke of the experience until nearly three decades later, when I was talking to my good friend Gail, who is clairvoyant. Several of Jen Weigel's Spiritual Social Club members were in attendance of her one-woman show, *I'm Spiritual, Dammit!* Gail must have intuitively sat next to me, which gave me the chance to ask the question that had been haunting me for decades.

"Gail, I've been wanting to ask you a question."

"Sure."

"I had an experience where ..."

"It was your mom coming to say goodbye." Gail just shrugged as if she were answering my question, which never came out of my mouth and was still stuck in my bewildered mind.

Now looking back on that entire experience nearly thirty years ago, it turns out Mom, who is now on "the other side," might have had a greater plan forming in her crystal ball of wisdom when she was alive. I just didn't see it coming. My mom introduced me to a psychic medium. This wasn't my cup of coffee at the time, but my mom convinced me, in the way most moms can accomplish this feat. And yes, the encounter was partly playful, partly terrifying, and mostly mind-blowing. And ultimately, it would become a tool for us to communicate in the spirit realm.

Spiritual Summary

Don't wait until someone's gone to tell them how much they mean to you, because that guilt and regret will eat you alive when it's too late to tell them; trust me, I know. The people we love don't stop loving us just because they've left their bodies; sometimes they show up as inexplicable light under your door the very night they pass, even when you're too scared and ashamed to let them in. And here's the kicker: Your loved ones on the other side are often working on plans you can't see yet, planting seeds while they're alive that won't make sense until decades later. Love transcends death, and the connections we think we've lost are often just waiting for us to be ready to receive them again.

The Chain-Smokin' Coffee Psychic

In June 1992, my mom and some of her hospital friends heard about a woman in Morris, Illinois, who was supposedly a psychic. By all accounts, a freaking accurate psychic at that. After Mom's visit, she insisted I needed to see this woman. Apparently, this psychic had told my mom several things about me that were spot-on, which is either impressive or creepy, depending on how you look at it. I'll let you decide for yourself. I'd never seen or spoken to a psychic before, so I figured, what the hell? Let's see what this lady's got. Maybe she'd tell me I was destined for greatness. Maybe she'd tell me to avoid seafood on Tuesdays. Who knows? As the time for my appointment drew closer, I became a little less enthusiastic about the whole thing. I didn't want to go through this mystical moment alone. What if she told me I was cursed or something? I needed a freak-show wingman. So I coerced my buddy Kevin (a.k.a. Noonie) into tagging along. As part of his agreeing to share in this experience, I told Noonie that I would take care of it for him, and all he needed to do was show up at the house, and we would drive there together. Noonie was also my insurance policy, in the event things got too trippy for me as well.

The day finally came to visit Carla, the coffee psychic. Yes, she read coffee grounds. No, I'm sorry, I don't know how that works either. Noonie showed up, said hello to my mom with a nervous smile that screamed, "What the hell have I gotten myself into?," and off we went to Morris to meet our fate. I was half expecting to pull up to something out of a horror movie, you know, a creaky old Victorian mansion, dead trees, maybe a few rotting birds or something like that for added effect. Instead, we found a regular four-story apartment building. The kind you'd find in any town. The kind where people have regular jobs and everyday lives and, apparently, the addition of one coffee-reading psychic. As we walked up the stairs, we kept looking at each other and giggling. It wasn't like we were telling jokes or anything; we were in full-on-flop-sweat, nervous-laughter mode. You know, when you're so uncomfortable, your body just decides to laugh at inappropriate times because it doesn't know what else to do with all that shit you're experiencing. My mind was racing as we walked down the long, stained-carpeted hallway that had clearly seen better days. What was her place going to look like? Was she going to have a crystal ball? Or . . . maybe she was wearing some sort of fortune-teller getup? Maybe she'd have chicken feet nailed to her wall to ward off evil spirits? (Is that even a thing, or did I make that up from some movie?) What am I doing? This is fucking nuts!

We finally reached the door at the end of the hallway. Cue the blank expressions and head tilts. Our not-so-sophisticated nonverbal communication system that basically meant, "You knock." "No, *you* knock." We stood there doing our *Night at the Roxbury* head bob thing until I broke the silence and said, "Oh, fuck it!" and knocked. Seconds later, the door flew open, and there she was: Carla, the coffee psychic lady. Carla looked nothing Jing like I'd envisioned. No warts on her nose, no flowing mystical robes, no ginormous crystal jewelry that allowed her to communicate with other dimensions. She was slender, blond, with shoulder-length hair and a warm smile.

She looked like my hot neighbor Bonnie. (It's not that kind of book, so we're gonna move on.) Oh, but there was one detail that became overwhelmingly evident: Carla was a smoker. Not just any smoker, a *chain* smoker. The kind who lit the next cigarette with the dying embers of the current one, which she did, by the way! She invited us into her apartment, and before she could finish asking who wanted to go first, Noonie made a beeline to the door. "Just come out when you're done," he said, not even turning around. The door slammed, leaving me alone with Carla, an overflowing ashtray, and three emergency packs of Marlboro Lights. There I sat at an octagonal glass-top kitchen table (because apparently regular tables aren't mystical enough), watching Carla light another cigarette and pull a deck of cards from her back pocket.

"Okay, tell me when to stop," she said, shuffling the cards.

"Stop what?"

"To stop shuffling the cards!"

"Oh, yeah . . . stop."

Look, this was my first psychic rodeo, mind you, and I was about to enter the arena with Chain-Smokin' Carla, the badass psychic bull staring me down.

"Okay, what would you like to know?"

"Can you tell me the winning lottery numbers?" I said with a laugh.

"Nope, it don't work that way."

"Doesn't," I mumbled, because apparently even in the presence of an "all-knowing psychic," I'm still a grammar dick. My internal voice immediately said, *"Shut up, dude. She could hex you or something, and then you're really screwed."*

"Um . . . okay, can you tell me if I'm going to meet someone and get married, you know, that sort of thing?"

Carla split the deck and laid out seven cards, each flip accompanied by a knowing "hmm . . . uh huh," as if she were examining an x-ray of my soul.

Then she let me have it: "You're going to marry a woman who knows your mom, and you're going to have one child, a son . . . from that marriage."

"From that marriage? What does that mean?"

"That marriage ain't gonna last long, but the next one, you'll be in for the long haul."

"Holy shit, that makes it sound like a prison sentence or something!"

Her face said everything, but her mouth didn't move, and that internal voice went off again: *Just shut up, man!*

"You're gonna have two children in that marriage. All boys. Three boys total. Hey, you want me to read the coffee for you?"

"Ah . . . yes, that would be great." So much for the card reading; maybe she was trying something new out on me.

"I'll be right back."

Carla left the room with two lit cigarettes in her hands and popped into the kitchen to get some coffee and creamer. Again, I have no idea what the significance of any of this stuff is. I wasn't familiar with the reading of coffee; hell, I didn't even drink much coffee at that time. Carla returned to the table quickly, with a cup of coffee in one hand, a carton of half-and-half creamer in the other, and one cigarette hanging from her mouth. (Hopefully the other ciggy butt didn't drop into her coffee.) Based on the expression on her face, the smoke must have been stinging her eyes. One eye was watery and red, while the other had a steely squint to it. I didn't ask her what the significance was with the creamer; quite honestly, I didn't want her to think I didn't know what was going on. Which, of course, I had no clue.

As she sat down, she immediately began to stare at the black coffee intently, then she began to rock back and forth ever so slightly. What started as a slight movement soon became a nearly bow-like motion. To say I was a little freaked out would be an understatement. Then there was an abrupt stop, at which point she took the carton of cream in her hands and lifted it to eye level, and started to slowly circle the coffee cup with the creamer. She only did this a few times and proceeded to pour the creamer into the cup. Then her gaze lifted, and she gave a nod, staring in my direction, but the nod wasn't intended for me; it was a nod to someone who would have been standing to the right of me. There is a big but here, though: The big but was that there was no one in her apartment but Carla and me.

Carla said, "I'm gonna open up to spirit, and people will be coming in to share things. Some things will be in the future, and some are from your past. I don't know who they'll be, but they'll come quickly.

"There's a person, a young man, reddish hair, he keeps popping in like he's playing hide-and-seek or something, he says his name is Tad, or ... something like that."

"Todd, that's my buddy Todd."

"He's nodding his head yes, Todd, it's Todd."

"Todd says he loves you and checks in on you often; he's really a funny guy, a jokester."

"Yep, that's Todd-O."

"He says he fu— He's telling me to say what he said, so here goes, he said he fucks with you from time to time, just to see if he can make you laugh. He hides your keys, your wallet, and your smokes. I didn't know you smoked; you could have smoked while you were here. I don't mind. He also says he loved the song you wrote about him, he says it's cool, even though he doesn't like hick music. Does that make sense? Did you write a song about him?"

"Yeah, I did."

"Well, he likes it, but what's hick music?"

"It's a country song called 'The Last Ride.' I used his nickname, which he got from where he grew up, in Toluca, Illinois: Dutch. It was more metaphorical; our last ride, which we all took together, was to Florida. We went out to sit on the beach in Fort Myers, Florida, and stared up at the stars. He was already sick then, so it took a lot out of him, but you'd never know it by the expression on his face. He soaked in every second of that trip; I only wish I did the same. I guess I was in denial. I didn't want to believe he was going to die from it. I kept thinking that if I ignored it, it would go away, but it obviously didn't."

"Sick?"

"Yeah, Todd-O had AIDS and died February 11, 1992. I really miss him."

"He says, 'You don't have to miss me, you big dope, I'm here and around you all the time . . .' He's gone."

WTF?! All I could think at that moment was WTF, and how in the hell did she know about Todd, and the song I wrote; this can't be real. Carla's head dropped down to her coffee cup, and a few seconds later, her eyes turned toward me again.

She then said, "A man is coming through, an older man, maybe a grandpa or someone like that. Do you have a grandpa who passed?"

"My great-grandpa passed away a long time ago."

"He's shaking his head, no."

"I don't have a grandpa who passed away."

"He's nodding his head yes, so he's saying you do."

"Hmm . . . I can't." With my shoulders slumping forward and my gaze dropped to the mystical cup of coffee on the table, I quickly realized that Carla was talking about my dad's dad, my Grandpa Alstott.

"He's just standing there, he hasn't said anything, he just . . . seems to be waiting for you to say something."

"Carla, I'm sorry, but I really don't have many good memories of him, and I would rather not hear from him or speak to him. I don't mean to be disrespectful, but I would rather move on and hear if you get any other information for me."

Carla's eyes returned to the coffee. This time, she was looking at the coffee differently, with a greater focus. This time, it was much more intense, almost as if she were watching a movie in her tiny ceramic cup. I couldn't help but find myself staring at Carla as intently as she was staring at the coffee cup. Her head and eyes were moving slowly, following something that was unfolding in that cup of java in front of her. All of a sudden, she leaped back away from the coffee, hitting the table with her leg, which happened to spill some of it. Then she just . . . stopped. The stop was abrupt and more than a little startling.

"What? What did you see? Am I gonna die?"

"We're all gonna die, that's not it."

"What is it, then?"

"Nothing . . . it's, it's, nothing."

Judging by the looks of things, it was definitely something. Carla was breathing as if she had just completed the anchor leg of a 400-meter relay, including a heaving chest and some shaking to boot. Keep in mind, she might plow through three packs of smokes on a light day, so take that with a grain of salt.

"Do you want me to take a look at anything else?"

"Nope, I'm good."

I couldn't wait to get the hell out of my seat and out in the hall. This was a lot to take in at the time. What the fuck just happened? What did she see? I was also thinking that Noonie may be halfway back to my house by now. I thanked her and let her know it was a great experience and that it was nice to meet her. I got up quickly and opened the door only to find a slightly pale-faced Kevin, who said, "What happened? Hey, don't go too far away, I don't want to be in there with this chick for too long." I offered to go in with him, but he quickly turned down my offer and went in to see what the fates had in store for him.

Wow, that was something, not just something, but a lot of something, so much information she was sharing with me, and how could she know all of that? Keep in mind, the internet wasn't much of a thing back then, if anything, really. As I leaned against the wall, my body began to feel shaky and weak, and I slid down the wall until I came to rest on the floor. There I was, alone again, lost in the thought of what had happened, rehashing everything that had just happened and what was said. For the life of me, I couldn't wrap my mind around the fact that this petite woman in Morris, Illinois, had all of this information. Then the how piece of the equation set in, how did she have all of this information? Who gave her this information? It made no sense at all. I was jolted out of my magical mystery tour of thoughts when the door flew open, and I saw Noonie speed-walking down the hallway, as if invisible demons were chasing him; his "Okay, let's go . . . *now!*" echoed behind him. Okay, I guess it's time to go. Noonie was way ahead of me, so when I got to the car, Kevin was already buckled in, staring straight ahead like he'd seen the exact date and time of his demise, careful not to make eye contact with me.

"You okay?"

"Yep. Let's go. Let's go now."

I couldn't help but laugh. My little buddy was clearly spooked, but no matter how many times I asked him what Carla said, the answer was always: "Nothing. I'm fine. Drop it." Now, if your closest friend was acting like they'd just been told they were going to be murdered by evil circus clowns, and was telling you to "Drop it!," would you drop it? Hell no! So for the entire hour-and-five-minute drive home, I remained steadfast in my mission to irritate the shit out of my friend and kept asking in the same monotone voice, "What did she say?—Drop it!—What did she say?—Drop it!—What did she say?"

Until, finally: "Will you just shut the fuck up already?"

That, my friends, was my first experience with a psychic medium, and the kicker: She was right about so many things. About the family, my boys, and my career, all of it. Pretty freaking cool, even if we did have to smoke three packs of Marlboro Lights in the hour we spent with Carla.

To this day, Noonie still avoids the subject and won't tell me what she said. My editor for this book had asked me if my friend had ever told me what was said, at which point I told him that we had spoken of it fairly recently, and there was still no offer to share what Carla had said. At his urging, I reached out via text, thinking it might be easier for him to share that way rather than having to speak the words, and this is what he said:

Me: Hey, bud, my editor said he'd really like to know what Carla said and asked if you wouldn't mind sharing it with us.

Noonie: Shut up. Tell your editor to F-off. Save it maybe for book 2.

Me: Ok, how about this? Did what she said come true?

Me (the next day): You never answered my question, brother.

Noonie (a day and a half later): Ya, some.

Some secrets, apparently, are worth taking to the grave . . . or at least until book number two. My guess is that Noonie won't be seeing another medium anytime soon. For me, quite the opposite—I now have a handful of friends who are mediums and I've been blessed to have been connected with my mom many times, as well as other loved ones.

Spiritual Summary

Your first encounter with the other side doesn't always come wrapped in mystical robes and crystal balls; hell, sometimes it shows up in a smoke-filled apartment in Morris, Illinois, with a chain-smoking blond who reads coffee grounds and knows shit about you that she has no business knowing. When someone from the other side shows up to tell you they're still around and they still love you, it doesn't matter how it happens or how weird the messenger is. What matters is that you pay attention. And if your buddy won't tell you what the psychic said to him thirty-plus years later, you can bet your ass it was accurate. That first reading cracked open a door I had never been through, and it's been swinging open wider ever since.

You Are the Medium You're Looking For

'd like to ask you to take a moment right here and right now. If you have a loved one who has passed away and you miss them, I'd like you to take a moment to share whatever is in your heart that you'd like to share. By the way, you don't need a psychic medium to talk to your departed loved ones; you can do it yourself. They now know things that we don't, like that their soul and energy are still here with us, and that they never left and they're perhaps nearer to us now than they were while they were here on Earth. This is pretty heavy stuff, so I understand if you're a little skeptical about all of it, but hang in there with me. I'd like you to take a moment to think about a loved one who is no longer with you on Earth and imagine that person sitting across from you.

Now, think of a happy memory you had with this person, and how much spending time with them meant to you, and how much you loved being with them. The next thing may not be so easy, but I'd like you to imagine what you might say to them if they were, in fact, sitting across from you. I'd like you to tell them exactly how you feel about them, and how much you love them, and what an important part of your life they were. I'd like you to take a minute or two, or however long you'd like to take in this moment and come back to the book. I'll be right here when you return, don't worry.

Okay, did you feel anything? Did you hear their voice, or see their smile? How about their laugh? Did you hear them? Chances are you did and a whole lot more. The next item on your to-do list, the soul work, if you will, is easier for some and might be the most difficult for others. I'd like you to reach out to a person who's still with us on Earth and call or text them. Just let that person know you wanted to send them love and were thinking of them. Do it right now; don't wait. There is no reason to wait. Right now is the perfect time to tell them what you genuinely feel; you never know when you won't have the opportunity to say it to them again. I'll be here when you get back.

Spiritual Summary

Don't wait to tell the people you love that you love them. Don't let pride, stubbornness, or the illusion that you have all the time in the world keep you from expressing what's in your heart. And if you've lost someone with words left unsaid, know this: Love transcends death, space, and time. The connection you had with that person didn't end when their body left the earth. Sometimes, if you're open to it, they'll find a way to let you know they're still there, still loving you and watching over you, more than ever before. But also know it's okay to be too broken up to receive that message right away. Grief is its own journey, and healing happens on its own timeline. And sometimes, time doesn't heal all wounds either, which is okay, too.

"I Can See Clearly Now":
Service to Others and
Expanded Consciousness

The natural progression from experiencing profound loss and prophetic knowing to helping others find their own path isn't something you plan—it just happens. Once you've experienced the depths of grief, the heights of spiritual connection, and everything in between, you can't help but want to share what you've learned. Not in a preachy "I see the light and you need to see it too" way, but with a genuine desire to help others who are struggling through the same shit storm you once knew so intimately.

"I Can See Clearly Now"
Johnny Nash

Johnny Nash had a song titled "I Can See Clearly Now," and boy did he have it right when he sang about seeing clearly after the rain has gone. Because, let me tell you, once you've done some serious spiritual healing work and start integrating all this new awareness stuff into your life, something weird starts to happen—you get this overwhelming urge to go out and help other people figure their shit out too. I'm not saying you run out onto a busy street corner with a megaphone and a sandwich sign, screaming at the top of your lungs about extraterrestrial beings. I'm also not talking about becoming some self-righteous spiritual guru who thinks they have all the answers. What I'm talking about is that natural pull you feel when you see someone struggling with the same stuff you used to struggle with, and you just want to reach out and say, "Hey, I've been there, and there's a way through this mess."

It's like when you finally figure out how to use some complicated software program, and then you can't help but show everyone else how to do it. Instead of teaching people how to program their $1,200 TV remotes that tell you when you're thirsty or have to use the bathroom, you're sharing tools for healing childhood trauma and connecting with their higher selves. You can see that there are slightly different stakes involved here. This monumental shift from focusing on the healing of your own bumps, bruises, and trauma to wanting to serve others isn't something you force—it's just something that happens naturally. One day, you're doing your own inner work, meditating, communicating with your guides or your higher self. The next thing you know, you find yourself in conversations where you're sharing what you've learned, offering to send someone a meditation, or just being that person who listens without providing solutions or casting judgment when someone needs to talk about their spiritual experiences. I have to say, I would have never imagined that I would be writing this book, but I've turned my experiences and pain into something I hope is useful to you. If there is one thing that you take away from this book that is helpful to you, then I have accomplished precisely what I set out to do.

For me, this stage started showing up in random ways. I'd be talking to someone about their struggles, and suddenly I'd hear myself sharing something Kelly, or another spiritual mentor, had taught me. Or maybe it could be describing a healing technique that had worked for me. I wasn't trying to be anyone's spiritual teacher; this new way of being was just that—it was new, and I am no expert—I was just sharing what had helped me survive the shit storm and begin to thrive. You may find this interesting, and honestly, really flipping strange. As you continue down this spiritual path, your consciousness begins to expand in ways that have you questioning everything you thought you knew about reality. I'm talking about those moments when you feel connected to something so far beyond your comprehension that it defies logic, and it's almost overwhelming. You start having these experiences, little things at first, that your rational mind can't quite categorize. Maybe you just "know" things that there's no way you should know. Maybe you have dreams that are so lucid that they feel more real than waking life. Or maybe you're sitting in a quiet meditation, and you suddenly begin to understand how everything in the universe is interconnected. It makes perfect sense, even though you can't explain it to save your life.

Speaking of lucid dreams, I would like to share a dream I had that is just as vivid to me today as it was when I experienced it. This dream came at a crucial time in my life and perfectly illustrates how expanded consciousness can provide us with guidance we desperately need but don't yet understand.

Spiritual Summary

Once you've done the healing work and started seeing clearly, you get this overwhelming urge to help other people figure their shit out, too. Not by screaming on a street corner with a megaphone, but through that quiet pull you feel when you recognize your old struggles in someone else's eyes. You don't have to be anyone's guru or pretend you have all the answers; sometimes service just looks like sharing a meditation that helped you or being the person who listens without judgment when someone needs to talk about experiences they can't explain. And as you keep walking this path, your consciousness starts expanding in ways that have you questioning everything you thought you knew about reality, which is weird as hell, but also kind of the point. You turn your pain into purpose, and suddenly all that suffering starts to make sense.

A Prophetic Dream About "Big 4-0"

It was in 1999 that my then-wife, Marisue, and I were trying to get pregnant, and when we ultimately did, of course, we were excited and began the usual planning and preparations that new parents typically do. We painted what would become the nursery and purchased a crib, mattress, dressers, and other essential baby items. We did all of this after announcing to everyone that we were going to have a blessed addition to our newly created family. My wife had noticed she had a hard spot on her breast, so she made an appointment with her doctor to get it checked out. Well, like most doctors, at least in Illinois, there was a bit of a wait—a nearly four-week wait. Marisue finally went in for her appointment, and the doctor felt that it would be a good idea to perform a needle biopsy, just as a "precautionary" measure. It's no surprise that the evening before the biopsy appointment wasn't all that restful. Thankfully, Marisue fell asleep quickly; she was exhausted. I, on the other hand, just kept going over everything in my mind. Something told me not to get online and start looking shit up because all it would do is send my brain spiraling more than it already was, but in typical fashion, that's precisely what I did. When I came back to bed, I honestly don't know if I fell asleep or simply passed out; all I can say is that I had a dream that was not only trippy as all get-out, but also slightly prophetic.

In my dream, I was in a field—the kind of field I was surrounded by as a kid growing up in Plainfield, Illinois, a cornfield with a grassy meadow that was carved out into different sections. With the fields came the usual scents; I could smell fresh-cut grass, the sweet fragrance of corn, manure, and a hint of potential rain in the air. In the distance, I could see a barn, no animals or anything, just an empty storage barn. As I walked toward the barn, the familiar colors and feeling of a nightmare began to appear and take shape. The sky, which started as clear, blue, and bright, began to darken. The familiar thick, murky green of my nightmares started to roll in like a fog; it was overpowering, and along with the dark, foreboding colors came the acrid smells and metallic taste that signaled the approach of a severe storm. As the winds picked up, I saw the clouds building and darkening on the horizon, and they began dropping toward the ground. You know the clouds I'm speaking of, right? The clouds in movies where all hell is about to break loose, and you can do nothing to stop it. As I continued my walk toward the barn, I saw a nun standing there. A nun? Sure, doesn't everyone dream of a nun standing and staring up at stormy skies?

As I approached the nun, I reluctantly said, "Don't you think we should find some shelter? It looks bad right now, and I think a tornado might be forming." My words weren't acknowledged; the nun continued to stare out at the stormy skies, her face frozen and expressionless. So I repeated myself, this time yelling to be heard over the howling winds, "Don't you think we should find some shelter? It looks bad right now; it looks like a tornado is forming!" No sooner did the words come from my mouth, it was happening: All hell was breaking loose. I could now see not one, but two tornadoes touch down and start barreling their way toward us. As I looked around frantically for shelter, I saw a white canoe on the side of the barn. The nun stood still, like an alabaster statue, staring at the ominous, murky-green sky. I gently grabbed the nun's arm and said, "We have to go; we have to go now!" As I led her toward the canoe, I said, "Sister, get under the canoe." The sister just stared up toward the sky, as if she hadn't heard a word I said. Once again, I yell, "Please, Sister, get under the canoe; we'll be safe here." At this point, the screaming of the wind was beyond deafening; I couldn't hear or think, and I could barely see. I just felt fear, and the metallic taste of the storm filled my mouth and nostrils. I screamed to her, "Sister, we need to get under the canoe. The tornadoes are coming straight for us, and if we don't do it now, we are both going to die!"

It's as if the sister were in a trance; she stood perfectly still, like a lighthouse braving the storms of the Atlantic, but this time, the sister responded. I couldn't hear her due to the storm's roar, but I could see her lips moving. I grabbed the sister by both arms and said, "We have to get under the canoe, *now!*" I grabbed the sister, along with the canoe, and covered us. I was petrified; I had never been in a tornado before, and this was complete chaos. The canoe felt as though a giant were trying to rip it from my hands. I didn't know how much longer I could hold on to this little white lifeline; my strength was nearly gone. The nun was still expressionless, looking toward the sky, but I saw her mouthing something. What was she saying? Was she praying or reciting the rosary? "Sister, what are you saying?" I couldn't hear her; the tornadoes were too close, nearly on top of us. I yelled again, like my life depended on it, "What did you say?!"

The sister turned and looked me in the eyes and said, "I said nothing is stronger than Big 4-0."

This time, I heard her; I heard it; I listened to what she said, but what in the hell does that mean? What does "nothing is stronger than Big 4-0" mean? So, still looking her in the eyes, I yelled, "What, what does that mean?!"

Again, she yelled, "Nothing is stronger than Big 4-0!" Nothing is stronger than Big 4-0; that doesn't make any sense. What is Big 4-0, and what does Big 4-0 have to do with anything?

As I mouthed what I had just heard, the sister did as well. As we looked at each other, we continued to repeat the nonsensical phrase "Nothing is stronger than Big 4-0" over and over, as if it were an ancient chant or a mantra: "Nothing is stronger than Big 4-0! Nothing is stronger than Big 4-0! Nothing is stronger than Big 4-0!"

And as quickly as the tornadoes were on top of us, they were gone—they disappeared as our chant ended. This chant, this crazy-ass, no-sense-making chant, is that what made the tornadoes go away? Was the chant the reason we were alive? I didn't know, and at that point I didn't care. As we crawled out from under the now mud-splattered canoe, I turned to the sister and asked, "What does 'Nothing is stronger than big 4-0' mean?"

With the slightest grin, the sister looked me in the eye and said, "My child, nothing . . . is stronger . . . than Big . . . 4 . . . 0 . . . !" She then pointed toward the heavens. When she pointed, my eyes naturally followed. It was then that I had one of those full-body convulsions, the type that jolts you out of a sound sleep. As I lay there, the only thing I could think about was that dream. What did the dream mean, and why a nun, a canoe, and a barn? It almost sounds like one of those bad jokes about a man, a horse, and a monkey walk into this bar and . . .

Marisue and I did get out of the house and made it to the appointment on time. While I sat there waiting for her return, I couldn't shake the feeling I had from the dream. What in the hell was the significance of the tornadoes and the nun, and what in God's name did "My child, nothing is stronger than big 4-0" mean? The needle biopsy appointment was finished, and that was the start of many more doctor's appointments that lay ahead of us. Marisue was in fact diagnosed with stage 4 (metastatic) breast cancer. She had a radical mastectomy and went through a full course of chemotherapy, and we were able to keep the baby, which many doctors advised against. We were spectators of what became a virtual parade of doctors, all of whom unanimously said that the pregnancy should be terminated, and aggressive chemo and radiation treatments should begin. Unanimously, except for one doctor. This doctor said there were options other than terminating the pregnancy, which we took. Although being six-and-a-half weeks early, a healthy Jonathan Edward Alstott was born on August 8, 2000. There is so much more to the story—maybe it will come out in my next book—but for now, this is what you get. I didn't know what "Nothing is stronger than Big 4-0" meant until years later, as you can see in the pictures at the end of this section; however, I eventually discovered at least part of its meaning. Big 4-0 might have been a what, but I know for sure, it was also a who. I believe Big 4-0 was God's way of telling me there was no need to worry; I'm here with you, and I've got this—trust in Me.

Big 4-0 has been a not-so-subtle reminder for me over the years, starting with my oldest son, and continuing with my other two boys, Nicholas and Brady. Nick and Brady are from my wife, Becky. Each of my boys donned the number 40 at some point in their athletic careers, and one still wears it on his baseball uniform today. God also blessed me with three amazing young men, whom I am thankful for every day. When I look at my boys, it's almost as if I'm looking into God's eyes, and He's looking back at me. Keep in mind that Jonathan was not supposed to be here with us, and by trusting my/our intuition, the right choice was made. Seeing a little piece of God in each one of my boys' beautiful eyes always makes me smile.

I realize that this dream might sound like I ate something that didn't agree with me or I drank too much, but this was one of many prophetic dreams I've had in my lifetime. I would be willing to bet some of you have had a prophetic dream or two that you've dismissed over the years as well. For a time, this was the only way I would receive "messages" or information. Some people's signs or messages come to them when they're awake, which must be a pleasant surprise when it happens.

Spiritual Summary

Sometimes the universe sends you messages wrapped in dreams so bizarre they sound like the setup to a bad joke . . . a nun, a canoe, and a tornado walk into a cornfield, and you'd swear you ate something that didn't agree with you. But here's the thing: Those nonsensical messages often turn out to be God's way of saying, "I've got this, trust Me," even when every logical voice around you is screaming to do the opposite. Prophetic dreams aren't always comfortable or clear, but if you pay attention and trust what you're being shown, you might just end up with miracles you were told were impossible. The meaning might not reveal itself for years, but when it does, you'll realize the universe was preparing you for this moment all along.

Top left: Nick, Jonathan, and Brady; **Top right:** Jonathan and me
Bottom left: Brady; **Bottom right:** Brady and Nick

Expanding into Service

The prophetic dream about Big 4-0 taught me something profound about expanded consciousness—it's not just about receiving information for ourselves. Sometimes we're given these insights to help others, to be of service in ways we couldn't have imagined. I have always been of service to others; it's seemingly just a part of who I am at my core. This sometimes makes it difficult to articulate effectively, which is why I chose to refer to someone I feel is the queen of expanded consciousness in this section.

My close friend Dr. Julie Foster, MD, wrote a book entitled *Remembering Awake: How to Play Creation with Y/our Soul*. In her book, Julie discusses the God particle, which is present in every single one of us, and how we are all interconnected. Julie is a bright light and the person I lovingly refer to as a tsunami of loving energy. Her book is truly remarkable, delving deeply into numerous healing practices that encompass both the physical and spiritual aspects of healing. I will also tell you that there's something about the audiobook, which she narrates herself, that feels comforting and will calm you almost immediately. I highly recommend that you listen to and/or read her book; you won't regret it. I used to think people who spoke of "universal consciousness" and "higher self" were either nuts or trying to slip something into my drink, and I would find myself waking up in some cave with people holding torches, wearing hooded robes, and chanting some shit in different tongues. When you start experiencing these expanded states of awareness for yourself, you realize that our normal, everyday consciousness is like looking at the world through a keyhole, and suddenly someone opens the door and yells, "Come on in!"

Here's the weird part, though. These experiences don't make you feel crazy at all; it's just the opposite—they make you feel more sane than you've ever felt in your life. It's like finally getting glasses when you didn't even realize you needed them. Everything becomes clearer, more connected, and more meaningful. Your intuition goes from being this tiny little whisper that you simply ignore to being this loud, clear voice that's right way more often than it's wrong. Synchronicities also start happening so frequently that you stop calling them coincidences and start paying attention to the messages they're bringing. And the really mind-blowing part? As if your mind wasn't already blown. You start to realize that serving others and expanding your consciousness aren't separate things at all—they're actually one and the same. The more you help others heal and awaken, the more you awaken, and your awareness expands. It's as if the universe has a built-in conveyor belt, where the more you put on the belt, or give, the more you receive. Spiritual growth is the same damn thing; it's a never-ending flow of loving energy.

I'm not going to lie—sometimes this expansion-of-consciousness thing can be overwhelming as hell. There are days when you feel like you're seeing and feeling way too much; it's like you need to find the volume knob for your spiritual awareness stereo and turn that shit down a notch. But then you realize that this expanded awareness is exactly what allows you to be of true service to others, because you can see and feel things that help you understand what they're going through on a deeper level. This whole being of service in the spiritual sense basically means helping others without keeping score or expecting a celestial gold star—it's like being the universe's personal assistant, except you get paid in good vibes and soul growth. Whether it's helping your neighbor carry groceries in from the car, volunteering at a food pantry, or actually taking the time to listen when someone talks instead of waiting for your turn to speak, it's all about doing good stuff because it's the right thing to do. You don't do it because you want recognition or a pat on the back.

Many spiritual traditions have different names for this—Christians call it "serving others," Hindus call it "sevā"—but it all boils down to this: Help people freely, don't be a dick about it when you do, rinse and repeat. The idea is that by serving others, you're actually developing your spiritual muscles like compassion, kindness, and generosity, while others believe you're also serving the Divine by taking care of "Its" creation (kind of like walking God's dog while He's busy running the universe). The beautiful part? It can be something as simple as sending an encouraging text or something as big as mission work in a foreign country—the universe doesn't care about how grand the gesture is, just the size of the heart that's behind it. The bottom line is: Spiritual service is basically recognizing that we're all connected, so helping others is really just helping yourself with a few added steps . . . and better karma.

The service aspect isn't about becoming some enlightened guru with all the answers. It's about being a wounded healer who's done enough of their own work to hold space for others to do theirs. It's about showing up authentically and saying, "I don't have it all figured out, but I've learned some things that might help." And the expanded consciousness thing? It's not about floating around in some blissed-out spiritual state all the time. It's about being able to access different levels of awareness when you need them—whether that's for your own healing, to understand someone else's journey, or simply to navigate life with a little more wisdom and compassion.

The combination of service to others and expanded consciousness creates a beautiful feedback loop. The more you serve, the more your consciousness expands. The more your consciousness expands, the more effectively you can serve. It's the universe's way of ensuring that spiritual growth benefits not just the individual but the collective. And that understanding leads naturally into the next stage of awakening—learning to trust the intuitive guidance that comes with this expanded awareness.

Spiritual Summary

When your consciousness starts expanding, you don't lose your mind—you finally find it. Prophetic dreams, knowing things you shouldn't know, and feeling connected to something beyond comprehension aren't signs you're going crazy; they're signs you're waking the hell up. The weird part is that the more your awareness expands, the more you want to help others expand theirs, and the more you help others, the more your own consciousness grows. It's like the universe designed this beautiful feedback loop where serving others and expanding your awareness are the same damn thing. Trust the process, even when it feels overwhelming, because expanded awareness is exactly what makes you useful to other people on their spiritual journeys.

"A Matter of Trust":
Intuition and Guidance

The progression from expanded consciousness to fully trusting your intuitive guidance is like learning to walk all over again—except this time, you're walking with invisible legs that know exactly where to go even if you're blindfolded. After all the healing, the service to others, and the consciousness expansion, there comes a point where you have to decide: Am I going to trust this inner knowing, or am I going to keep second-guessing the very gifts that have saved my life more than once?

"A Matter of Trust"
Billy Joel

The ninth stage of Dolores Cannon's twelve stages of spiritual awakening is intuition and guidance. Several songs came to mind for this section: "Don't Stop Believin'" by Journey, "Believe" by Mumford & Sons, and "Faith" by George Michael. However, the one that really hit the nail on the head for me is Billy Joel's "It's a Matter of Trust." Having this song come to mind for this section is no surprise; I have been a Billy Joel fan for most of my life. The song highlights trust as a fundamental component in relationships. Spiritually, this aligns with the idea that trusting others—and oneself—is essential to growth and connection. Trust can be seen as a spiritual practice that nurtures compassion and understanding and feeds your intuitive gifts. The most important thing about everything I've mentioned so far is the trust you must have in yourself and your intuition. I'll say that there are still times, even today, that I second-guess my intuition and try to brush it off as a coincidence. However, our intuition is never wrong. You always know, or as my good friend Jennifer Grace says, "YAK."

You can think of intuition as being much like a muscle group you're working out. You do chest and back on Monday and Wednesday, then move on to shoulders and arms on Tuesday and Thursday, and include an intuition and leg day on Friday. However, unlike other muscle groups, your intuition muscles can be exercised every single day. Much like anything else that you'd like to improve upon or become more proficient in, you need to work on refining your intuition as well. How do you do that, you may be asking? It's simple, but not easy. What makes it simple is the fact that your intuition is popping up all over the place, at any time of day. As a matter of fact, your intuition flows so much that it can become white noise to you, and you might simply ignore it. This is where the not-so-easy part comes in. Since we have determined that there is a constant state of flowing intuition and we look past it or through it, the difficulty is in stopping when you pick something up. You need to stop, take a breath, and listen and feel that intuition coming in. Since we have become patterned to ignore our intuition, you need to reprogram your brain to say, "Stop, look, and listen" to that voice that's giving you information you can use.

Now, there can be several situations that arise where your intuition kicks in, and your intuitive feelings can come in various forms. Some people get stomach aches. My friend Jenniffer Weigel is one who, as a child, was taken to the doctor by her mother, and I'm paraphrasing here, was told by the doctor that it was all in her head and that there was nothing wrong with her. Can you imagine what it must have been like to be a highly intuitive child, and your intuitive sign for something not being right was a stomachache? *And . . .* you go to a person who is supposed to be an authority on health and someone who is supposed to make you feel better, and they essentially say you're crazy and that it's all in your head? What the hell?! Unfortunately, I know Jen wasn't alone in this area; many of us "sensitive" people were often dealing with stomach issues, respiratory issues, allergies, etc. Some are even misdiagnosed as being bipolar as children.

Intuition is a gift that we all possess; however, many individuals have refined this gift to a level where they become intuitive practitioners. I'm fortunate enough to have a close friend who is a practicing intuitive; she goes by the moniker the "No-Nonsense Intuitive." Gail Alexander is a friend who possesses numerous spiritual gifts, earning her the nickname "Spiritual Swiss Army Knife." I should probably trademark that one, just in case. Gail's story is truly unique in that people often have one or two of their gifts emerge at a time; she happened to have all of hers appear simultaneously. In her books, Gail refers to this as being on "Mr. Toad's Wild Ride on acid." I mean this comment with the utmost love: Gail is like having a living, breathing spoiler alert as a friend. Her intuition is so refined that it's pretty freaking difficult to surprise her.

Another term that is often used when discussing intuition is claircognizance. As discussed earlier, this essentially means the ability for a person to acquire psychic knowledge without knowing how or why they know it. Think about this for a second . . . how many times have you been thinking about someone, and that someone just happens to be calling you while you were thinking of them? I bet it's happened to you more times than you can remember! It's that sort of thing that I'm talking about, and over time, you can develop your gifts or skills to impressive levels. Probably not to the level of the No-Nonsense Intuitive, honestly; Gail is a one-of-a-kind person. If you recall, Gail is the person who told me, just before the curtain rose on Jen Weigel's one-woman show, *I'm Spiritual, Dammit!*, that it was my mom who came to see me on the night she passed, without me having asked the question that was on my mind.

Overcoming skepticism and fear is crucial in the spiritual awakening process. Letting go of doubt and beginning to trust your intuition can further open your heart and mind, which fosters personal and spiritual growth. This aligns with Ms. Cannon's ninth stage, where a person might start to rely more on inner guidance and intuition, understanding that there's something or someone much larger at play.

Spiritual Summary

Your intuition is never wrong; you always know, even when you're busy talking yourself out of what you know. The trick isn't developing some mystical new ability, it's learning to stop treating the guidance that's been flowing through you your whole life like background noise and starting to pay attention to it. Trusting yourself and that inner voice might feel like learning to walk with invisible legs, but those legs have been saving your ass longer than you realize. So, maybe it's time to stop second-guessing them. Like any muscle, your intuition gets stronger the more you use it; the hard part is remembering to stop, breathe, and listen to what it's telling you.

"I'll Be There":
Pat Answered the Call

Little Michael Jackson said in his song, "I'll Be There," just call his name. I needed someone to help me make sense of things, and Pat Longo was there when I called. As you continue to develop your intuitive skills, you will find others in the field who are willing to share their gifts freely to assist you in your journey. What I mean is, some practitioners, such as Gail Alexander, are eager and supportive of people who are seekers and fledglings in this sort of practice and willfully provide guidance or suggestions to assist you in your "leveling up." But sometimes, the universe has to practically drag you by your ear to the teacher you need, especially when fear is holding you back.

"I'll Be There"
Jackson 5

Pat Longo was another such person. I had been in Jen Weigel's Spiritual Social Club for nearly a year when Jen suggested that I reach out to Pat to discuss her taking me on as a student, to further advance my intuitive skills. Pat was a renowned healer with a global following, who was so much more than a teacher of classes. Her unique gifts of healing were beyond conventional belief; they approached miracle status. These are my words and not those of Pat. She never considered herself the one who was responsible for the healing; rather, she considered herself to be the conduit of such miracles. She was able to heal people who, up until the point of meeting Pat, were considered to be in a hopeless situation. Simply by laying her hands on a person, Pat would transfer healing energies into the ailing client to provide them not only with relief from their pain, but actually heal them. Her abilities encompassed more than physical healings; Pat was probably best known for her capacity to heal crippling anxieties within people—people who couldn't even leave their homes for basic necessities. She even ended up authoring a book, *The Gifts Beneath Your Anxiety*, on how to release these seemingly life-altering afflictions.

Who in their right mind wouldn't want to meet a person who offered all of these amazing things, right? Pat had the requirement of being interviewed before you could attend her class. Being in the infancy stages of this new existence, I was, needless to say, a little nervous about meeting the person responsible for bringing to light such individuals as Teresa Caputo, Kim Russo, Heather Sprigg, Joseph D'Airo, Nick Lodato, and Nate Scripture, just to name a few. Those names are well known in the world of mediums, psychic mediums, and healers. I was by no means in their league, so I did what any chickenshit person would do and didn't reach out to Pat for almost another year.

I did finally reach out to her. Why? I'm not entirely sure, but my intuition told me I needed to reach out and schedule a session with Pat. The knowing, or feeling, I had was so strong that it was as if some invisible person were dragging me by the arm and wouldn't let me procrastinate any longer. I had actually planned on visiting friends in Long Island, New York, and tying in an in-person session with Pat. Four days before I was slated to leave, I ended up changing my plans and had to stay back in the Chicagoland area. It worked out well, though. Pat's assistant told me she wasn't in great health at the moment and that having the session via Zoom would ultimately be better for both of us. I had met Pat on a few different occasions via special Zoom sessions of the Spiritual Social Club but doubted she would remember me; after all, this was Pat Longo, teacher and mentor to world-famous mediums who had their own television shows, for crying out loud. Two weeks before the meeting, I had the opportunity to speak with Pat's assistant several times, which was part of the process. Her assistant also happened to be her sister, and Pat would have Eileen conduct the reconnaissance to ensure that there were no surprises or anything "weird" that might come up during the session. Eileen is an absolutely fantastic person, whom I enjoyed meeting and speaking with, and am honored to say she was happy to share the same sentiments with Pat about me.

When the day came to meet with Pat, I was a little nervous, but more excited than anything to have a one-on-one session with *the* Pat Longo. The Zoom window lit up, and there she was, Pat Longo, with a smile that filled the screen. With a smile on her face and in her voice, Pat said, "I knew it was you, Jim; your energy is unmistakable." Of course, the comment embarrassed me, and she could tell and immediately followed up with, "Everyone has their own unique energy signature, and I remembered yours from the Zoom classes you were in with me. It really is something."

We proceeded to talk and laugh for the next two hours and fifteen minutes, never once discussing what I wanted from the session or inquiring if there was a problem I needed to solve or a healing that needed to be done. Have you ever met someone that you felt so comfortable with, it felt as though you had known them for your entire life? If you have, this is how it felt while I was talking with Pat. Pat told me about being friends and classmates with Billy Joel, who happens to be one of my musical heroes, and how her husband, Vinny, accidentally stabbed Billy's hand with a steak knife one day after school, while they were wrestling around and rough-housing. She said Billy's mom was so mad that she chased Vinny out of the house. She also shared several other stories that kept a Cheshire Cat smile on my face the entire call. At about the two-hour-and-fifteen-minute mark, I slipped in the comment and question that had been a year in the making.

"Pat, Jen Weigel said that if I wanted to attend your classes, I needed to have some sort of interview with you . . ."

"Oh, honey, what do you think we've been doing all this time?"

Of course, I laughed again and said, "Well?"

"You have to attend my classes; your gifts are truly powerful, and your energy is through the roof! What would you like to get from joining our classes?"

"I'd like to refine my intuitive skills and receive messages or signs while I'm awake, rather than having to wait until I'm sleeping to get them."

"Oh . . . that's easy, we'll take care of that right away."

We talked for a few more minutes and probably would have kept going, but she said it was the third time her sister had called to remind her of her next appointment, and that we should wrap it up for this session.

Before we said our goodbyes, Pat let me know she was sending me a lot of homework to complete and a list of books she recommended that I read. I have included the following books, should you feel compelled to explore things further:

- *The Gifts Beneath Your Anxiety* by Pat Longo
- *Many Lives, Many Masters* by Dr. Brian Weiss
- *The Place Between Here and There* by Katherine Plant and Stephen Weber
- *The Wisdom of Florence Scovel Shinn* by F. S. Shinn
- *To Heaven and Back* by Dr. Mary C. Neal
- *Waking Jules* by Julie Clapp
- *Finding Emelyn* by Diane Richards
- *Angelspeake* by Barbara Mark & Trudy Griswold
- *There's More to Life than This* by Theresa Caputo

She also asked me to send her an email with a few days and times to continue our conversation. I, of course, emailed Pat and had the opportunity to meet with her for a couple more Zoom sessions, and I also attended two of her mediumship/intuitive classes. In our last Zoom session with each other, Pat mentioned something that didn't make much sense at the time, but now it's very clear. Pat had mentioned that no matter what happens, I needed to share my experiences with people and that it was equally important for it to come from a place of vulnerability, my authentic self, my voice. That was the last time I spoke with Pat before she passed. I certainly hope she would approve of sharing my experiences the way I have in this book.

I have one last story that involves Pat that I'd like to share with you. In July 2025, I accompanied my youngest son to a baseball prospect camp held at the University of Notre Dame. On the morning of the final day of the camp, we had a little extra time before things got started, so I suggested to my son that we visit the Grotto of Our Lady of Lourdes, located on the university campus. To my surprise, I got a "Sure, that sounds cool" from my son. The Grotto of Our Lady of Lourdes is a magnificent site on campus that is well worth visiting. The grotto is one-seventh the size of the French shrine where the Virgin Mary appeared to Saint Bernadette on eighteen occasions in 1858, which is likely one of the many reasons Father Sorin, founder of the University of Notre Dame, vowed to reproduce it on the campus. As we made our way to our destination, I told my son that we wouldn't be long; I just wanted to light a candle for Pat, her family, and our loved ones who had passed away. After lighting the candle and saying my prayer, my son and I started to leave. We only took a couple of steps when a cardinal flew directly in front of us and perched on a branch.

"Did you see that?" my son said.

"Yep, I sure did. Do you know what the spiritual significance of seeing a cardinal is when you're thinking of a loved one?"

I gathered by the vacant expression on his face, he didn't know. So, here's how I understand the meaning of seeing a cardinal when you're thinking of a departed loved one. Cardinals have been considered to be messengers from departed loved ones for a long time. Their presence is meant to be a sign that lets you know they're still with you. In many spiritual traditions, seeing a cardinal—especially a red one—is believed to be a sign that someone who has passed is nearby, watching over you. They symbolize hope, renewal, and the continuing connection between this world and the next. Then, as we reached the point to get on the main path to head back to the car, a white dove was sitting right in the middle of the path we needed to walk on. This is kind of cool too: white doves represent purity, peace, love, and connection with the divine. Guess what Pat's spirit animal was? That's right, Pat Longo was referred to by many as "the dove," so seeing a cardinal and a dove in that exact spiritual moment was pretty freaking amazing.

My son looked at me and said, "That's probably not a coincidence then, is it, Dad?"

"I don't think it is. There are a lot of people who believe that there's no such thing as a coincidence. I think I'm starting to lean into that way of thinking myself."

The appearance of both birds at that precise moment taught my son something that no amount of explanation could have accomplished—that spiritual signs are all around us, if only you keep your eyes open. It also lets us know that our departed loved ones find ways to communicate with us, and that trusting your intuition about these signs is part of the journey. Pat was still teaching her class, even from the other side.

Spiritual Summary

Learning to trust your intuition isn't just about developing psychic abilities—it's about learning to trust yourself on a whole new level. Your intuitive gifts are like muscles that get stronger by working them out, but the hardest part isn't receiving the information or signs, it's having the guts to listen and act on them. When you find mentors and teachers who recognize your gifts and encourage you to develop them, pay attention—these people don't show up by accident. And when you start seeing signs and synchronicities giving you that little wink that you're on the right path, like cardinals and doves appearing exactly when you need that little reassuring boost, trust that the universe is communicating with you in its own perfect way.

The Manifestation Stage:
"Every Little Thing She Does Is Magic" and "She's a Beauty"

The journey from trusting your intuition to discovering you can actually cocreate your reality is like going from being a passenger to realizing you've had access to the controls of the ship all along. After experiencing prophetic dreams, developing intuitive abilities, and learning to trust spiritual guidance, the manifestation stage arrives not as something new, but as a recognition of something you've been doing unconsciously your whole life.

"Every Little Thing She Does Is Magic"
The Police

"She's a Beauty"
The Tubes

"Every Little Thing She Does Is Magic" kept bouncing around my head like a pinball that wouldn't find its way out. Then the Tubes chimed in with "She's a Beauty," and suddenly I had a Spiritual Soundtrack I couldn't shake. Now, before you think I've lost my mind and decided to write a section about my make-believe love life—which would lead to a very uncomfortable conversation with my wife—let me explain how these songs perfectly capture what happens when you reach the manifestation stage of spiritual awakening. The manifestation stage is where shit gets real, and by real, I mean really freaking magical. This is where you start to understand that you're not just some helpless little victim of circumstance getting tossed around by life like a rag doll. You're actually a cocreator in this whole cosmic symphony, and your thoughts, feelings, and beliefs are literally shaping your reality.

Now, I know what you're thinking: "Oh great, here comes the woo-woo manifestation bullshit where Jim tells me to think positive, loving thoughts and unicorns will start shitting rainbows in my backyard." Not exactly. Though I have to admit, having a rainbow-shitting unicorn in your backyard would be kind of awesome. The manifestation stage isn't about sitting around visualizing a yellow Ferrari and waiting for one to suddenly appear in your driveway. It's about understanding that you've been manifesting your entire life—you just didn't know it; you weren't conscious of it. Every belief you hold, every emotion you consistently feel, every thought pattern you've been running on repeat—that's all been creating your reality. The only difference now is that you're becoming aware of the process.

Looking back now, I can see how my unconscious manifesting created years of struggle. When you spend decades believing you're destined to fail, guess what shows up? Failure after failure, perfectly manifested by a mind that didn't know it was creating its own reality. When Sting sings about finding magic in every little thing someone does, he's describing what happens when you shift into a high-vibrational state of gratitude and wonder. That's not just lovey-dovey fluff-stuff—that's manifestation 101. When you're genuinely grateful for what's already in your life, when you're seeing magic and beauty everywhere you look, you're sending out a vibrational signal that attracts more things to appreciate and find magical. It's like tuning your internal radio to the "holy shit, life is amazing" station, instead of the "everything sucks, and nothing ever works out for me" station. And trust me, I was a loyal listener to that second station for a lot of my life.

Oh, and don't let me forget, there's also this other vital piece to the whole manifestation thing. In metaphysical mumbo-jumbo boiled down, our frequency, let's call it our "inner state," is the vibrational catapult for our manifestations. So what the hell does this mean? Well, our outer reality is a direct reflection of our inner being. Manifesting gets much easier when we are in a healed, appreciative, and peaceful state. Sort of what I was talking about in those other sections. Here's a quick and easy rule to remember: The inside comes first, followed by the outside. It's my little cheat code I use when I'm trying to get a temperature check on my manifestations and my overall progress while humaning. The world outside mirrors back to me what I am experiencing internally. In this earthly dimension, though, our outer reality (or manifestations) takes a smidge more time to catch up with what's going on inside—so trust there's a little bit of buffer or lag, if that's what you want to call it. Kind of like a patchy dial-up internet connection to the universe, but you've got to first listen to all these squeaky, high-pitched, agitating, dissonant tones before you can get a clear signal.

The Tubes' "She's a Beauty" captures another crucial aspect of manifestation—the power of seeing perfection in what you desire. When you're looking at someone (or something), thinking they're beautiful, you're not focusing on their flaws or what's missing. You're seeing them through the lens of gratitude and appreciation. That energy of pure appreciation is like rocket fuel for your manifestation spaceship. During my spiritual awakening, I began to notice that when I genuinely felt grateful and appreciative—not just forcing it or faking it but truly feeling it—things started shifting in my life. Not always in the way I expected, but always in a way that served my highest good. Kelly Schwegel taught me about something called "vibrational alignment," which sounds like something you'd get done to your car, but it's actually about matching your internal energy to what you want to attract. When you're in a state of genuine appreciation, love, or excitement, you're vibrating at a frequency that naturally draws similar experiences to you. Think of the old saying: Birds of a feather flock together.

I remember working on manifesting better health (because let's be honest, at four hundred freaking pounds, I needed to supersize all the help I could get). Instead of focusing on how much I hated how I looked or felt, Kelly guided me to focus on appreciating what was working. My heart was still beating, my lungs were still working, I had use of all my limbs—basic stuff, right? But when I truly felt gratitude, genuine, authentic gratitude for these things, something shifted. It wasn't magical in the *Harry Potter* sense. I didn't wake up the next morning looking like Ryan Reynolds (though that might have been cool). But opportunities started presenting themselves. I met the right people at the right times. Information came to me when I needed it. Doors that had been closed to me before started opening up. It was as if the universe had started conspiring to help me, rather than me being the galactic doormat. What stood out to me most about this shift wasn't the external changes—it was realizing I'd spent fifty-plus years fighting against the current instead of learning to swim with it. The universe wasn't punishing me after all; I was just finally beginning to understand the rules of the game.

The manifestation stage taught me that thoughts become things, but not in the simplistic way a lot of self-help books make it sound. It's not just about thinking positive thoughts and wishing for things to happen—it's about aligning your entire being (thoughts, emotions, beliefs, and actions) with what you want to create. Don't let the key word slide by you now; action is the linchpin in this equation. Without an action step, you may as well be dreaming. And here's something else that blew my mind: You can't manifest from a place of lack or desperation. When you're trying to manifest money, for instance, because you're terrified of being broke, guess what happens? You're actually manifesting from the energy of fear and scarcity, which brings you more fear and scarcity and ultimately, more brokeness, if that's a word. When you're trying to manifest a relationship because you feel lonely and incomplete, you're manifesting from the energy of loneliness. However, when you can genuinely appreciate the money you already have (even if it's just a few dollars), when you can feel grateful for the relationships you already have in your life (even if it's just your dog or cat), when you can find beauty and magic in your current circumstances—that's when the real manifestation starts to happen.

This doesn't mean you have to pretend everything is perfect or have to fake being happy when you're not. It means finding authentic moments of appreciation and building on those. It means looking for evidence that the universe is actually working in your favor, rather than being a constant reminder that life sucks and the entire universe is against you. The manifestation stage also taught me about the importance of inspired action. That's right, there's that word again! You can't just sit on your couch, chanting and visualizing your dreams, and expect them to come knocking on your door. But when you're in vibrational alignment with what you want, you'll get intuitive hints about what actions to take. You'll feel inspired to call someone, go somewhere, or try something new. And when you do follow those inspirations, that's when the magic happens.

I've learned that manifestation isn't about controlling outcomes—it's about becoming the kind of person who naturally attracts what you desire. It's about embodying the energy of what you want before you actually have it. It's about finding the magic in every little thing, seeing the beauty in what's already here, and trusting that more beauty and magic are on their way. The coolest part about the manifestation stage is that it makes you realize you've been creating your reality all along. The difference is that now you're doing it consciously, with awareness and intention. You're no longer some random victim of fate—you're a deliberate creator, working in partnership with the universe to bring about what's in your highest good. And sometimes, just sometimes, when you least expect it, every little thing really does feel like magic.

My Manifestation Moment

There's a specific reason those songs came to me when describing manifestation. You see, there's a person who was the subject of my most powerful manifestation experience, and that story perfectly illustrates how manifestation works when you're truly aligned with what you're meant to receive. The person I'm referring to is a she, and I happen to feel that every little thing she does is magic and that she is truly one in a million. Let me share this magical manifestation story with you. So, there I was, like many late afternoons in the summer: wearing shorts, sunglasses on my head, earbuds in my ears, and a smile on my face. I can usually be found walking behind my dear old friend, my lawnmower. I had just finished listening to a book on Audible by Brian Weiss, called *Many Lives, Many Masters*, and a suggestion popped up that I give a listen to a book I hadn't heard of before. Why not? So I clicked on it and the download began. This book was written and narrated by an author I didn't know, but the last name was familiar to me; the book was *This Isn't the Life I Ordered* by Jenniffer Weigel. Weigel, I thought to myself, I wonder if she's related to the famous sportscaster Tim Weigel, who passed away from brain cancer. I shrugged, pushed play, and began to listen. Mowing away, row by row I went, listening intently to every word that was spoken. Laughing out loud, shaking my head, and smiling until my cheeks hurt. I wrapped up cutting the grass but continued listening to the book. I went to work out, basically so I could continue listening. I peeked my head in the door of the house and yelled, "I'm heading to the gym and will be back later," not listening for a response because it would surely disrupt the flow of the book I was in and had been for the past two hours and fifteen minutes. I arrived at the gym and proceeded to dawdle around so that I could listen to the book a little longer. After spending two hours at the gym, doing God knows what, I felt it was time to leave and head back home. By the time I returned, I had been listening to the book for nearly four and a half hours, which meant I only had two more hours of the book left.

So I did what any sane individual would do: I locked myself in my office and finished the book. The book by Jenniffer Weigel was nothing short of amazing. She was funny, relatable, and most of all, authentic. She used a familiar vocabulary consisting of some of my favorite words: Shit, damn, and the mother of all vulgarity, the F-bomb! That's right, this was my kind of person; she said fuck like nobody's business and didn't even apologize for it! Ms. Jenniffer Weigel was now officially my favorite author. The book was nothing short of amazing to me. The next morning, I received a call from my buddy Steve Stern (shout-out to Sterno), and he asked what I was doing. I said, "I'm looking for another book written by my new favorite author."

"Who's that?"

"Jenniffer Weigel, Jen Weigel."

"Huh, I know Jen Weigel, I went to the University of Illinois with her and used to hang out with her and her brother Rafer all the time."

"What?! You know Jen Weigel?"

"Yeah, why?"

"I have to meet this woman."

"Whoa . . . hahaha, what do you think your wife will say about that?"

"Not that way! She is . . . she is . . . she is going to be a friend of mine. I think she sounds like a person who would be awesome to hang out with and really get to know."

"Yeah, well, I don't have her number, so I can't help you with that. But if you do get in touch with her, ask her if she remembers Steve Stern."

"I will for sure."

"Hey, I have another call coming in and I gotta go, bye."

After we hung up, I wrote on a Post-it Note, "Get in touch with Jen Weigel." I'm going to meet Jen Weigel!

Now that I have made this proclamation, how exactly am I going to go about doing that? Well, while I'm trying to figure out what my master plan is, I'm going to listen to another one of Jen's books and get inspired. So that's precisely what I did. While I listened to *I'm Spiritual, Dammit!*, all I kept thinking was, I need to meet Jenniffer Weigel. The thought bounced around in my head like a proverbial BB in a boxcar and damn near became my mantra. What the hell was wrong with me? Why was I having this thought loop running in my head? This was starting to become weird, even for me! What I understand now is that this obsessive ADHD quality of mine wasn't me being a weirdo—it was my intuition trying to get my attention. When manifestation is working, it often feels like an internal GPS that won't shut up until you follow the directions. The universe was basically putting a giant neon sign in my head that said, "PAY ATTENTION TO THIS PERSON . . . MAKE A U-TURN AT THE NEXT STOP LIGHT."

I could see it now: me finally meeting Jen Weigel at some function for psychic mediums and walking up to her saying, "Hi, Ms. Weigel, my name's Jim Alstott, and you're my favorite author, and I made a t-shirt that says 'Jen Weigel's Biggest

Fan.' Here, look, I have it on under my dress shirt and tie." And that's when security would come bursting through the doors and escort me out while the ten o'clock news reported: "A rabid fan from Sugar Grove, Illinois, stalks Emmy Award–winning novelist and news anchor Jenniffer Weigel. Bob, now back to you."

Yeah, that turned freaky quickly! In all seriousness, though, I really felt the need to meet Jen, and I didn't know why. Then it happened. While listening to her book, she mentioned she had started a group for like-minded individuals to share a safe space to meet and discuss their spiritual adventures. Jen mentioned the Spiritual Social Club and continued with her narration. I had to look it up. There it was: the Spiritual Social Club! On jenweigel.com, I noticed a drop-down menu specifically for the club, and right next to it was another menu that read "Contact." I had to reach out to Jen. I entered the required information, and below that was a space for a message. I stared at this page for what might have been an hour, then I did the unthinkable: I wrote Jenniffer Weigel a note. After carefully crafting my email, being sure not to sound too much like an unhinged stalker fan, I pressed send. She'll never respond to my email. After all, this is *the* Jen Weigel, and I'm confident she doesn't have time to respond to a nobody like me. She's probably out writing another best-selling book or saving innocent lives somewhere around the globe, or at the very least, saving a poor kitten stuck in a tree.

Fast forward to the very next morning, and there it was: a response from Jen Weigel! I thought it was surely an automated response, but when I opened the email, I was dead wrong. Jen was very kind and welcoming in her email and suggested we get on a call to discuss my current spiritual journey and explore whether joining the Spiritual Social Club would make sense. That call took place in October 2023, and

Jen and I have been friends ever since. The interesting thing is that Jen has been a friend, a spiritual mentor and teacher, a sounding board, a facilitator in meeting others, and a staunch supporter of mine during this time. She was the first person to give me a loving and supportive kick in the ass to start writing this book after I told her about my book-writing dream.

The universe delivered precisely what I needed, not what I thought I wanted. I thought I was manifesting "meeting" my favorite author. What I actually manifested was finding a spiritual mentor, writing coach, podcast promoter, and the person who would help me birth this book you're reading right now. Sometimes the universe has bigger plans than we do. By the way, if you know me, you'd think that the notion of me writing a book was absolutely ridiculous; beyond that, you'd think it was utterly impossible. Don't get me wrong, I love listening to books; I listen to audiobooks all the time, in fact. The best thing I can come up with is that this must be something that my higher self, departed loved ones, or God Himself is involved with making happen. Whatever the reason, I'm grateful to have been allowed the opportunity to write this for all of you. As a matter of fact, at times it feels as though I was chosen to write this book.

Manifestation comes in countless shapes and sizes for us. Some people pray or say novenas. Others may write their manifestation down for five days, fifty-five times a day. The how isn't nearly as important as just doing it. Please know this: If I can do it, you can sure as shit do it, too.

The manifestation of meeting Jen Weigel taught me that when you're truly aligned with your purpose and following those intuitive nudges, no matter how crazy they seem, the universe will move mountains to make it happen. But . . . you have to take the inspired action—you have to write the email, make the call, show up. The magic is in the combination of intention, alignment, and action.

Spiritual Summary

Here's the thing about manifestation that most self-help books get wrong: You've been doing it your whole life. Yep, it's true, you just didn't know it. Every limiting belief, every fear, and every "nothing ever works out for me" thought has been creating your reality, whether you realize it or not. The difference now is you're awake to it, which means you can stop fighting the rip current and start swimming with it. But . . . manifestation isn't about sitting on your couch visualizing a Ferrari and waiting for it to magically appear in your driveway; it's about becoming the person who naturally attracts what serves your highest good by aligning your thoughts, emotions, and actions with genuine appreciation for what you already have. You see, the magic happens when you take inspired action from a place of gratitude rather than desperation, following those intuitive nudges even when they seem batshit crazy. And here's the kicker: The universe often delivers what you *actually* need, instead of what you thought you wanted. Which is how reaching out to your favorite author somehow turns into finding a spiritual mentor, a writing coach, and the loving kick in the ass you needed to write the very book you're holding—or, if you opted for Audible, the buttery voice currently whispering spiritual wisdom into your ears. You're welcome. Shameless plug.

Unity Consciousness:
"We Are the World" and "One Love"

Okay, I get it; you're probably thinking, "What the hell is Jim doing right now? Why is he suddenly throwing two songs at us for one stage?" Well, the truth is that several songs could resonate with people at this stage of their awakening. Since I have already set the precedent for mentioning two songs in the manifestation stage, I feel it's perfectly acceptable to do so again. Quite honestly, I could have probably listed twenty more songs, but these two have been rattling around my brain for quite some time, and it's time for them to get out of the old noggin and onto the page.

"We Are the World"
USA for Africa

"One Love"
Bob Marley and the Wailers

Please allow me to explain my reasoning. Have you ever found yourself at a party or, let's say, a professional conference, and you're having a conversation with someone, and it seems eerily familiar to you, almost like déjà vu? Then it hits you—it hits you like a bolt of lightning to the forehead—that you have been having the same conversation or disagreement with different people your whole life?

Welcome to unity consciousness, my friend—except instead of just recognizing patterns, you start understanding that maybe, just maybe, we're all connected in ways that would make your high school physics teacher, Mr. Hunt, cry tears of quantum joy. According to Dolores Cannon's spiritual roadmap, this is the stage where the whole "me versus them" wall starts tumbling down. Not in a Ronald Reagan "Mr. Gorbachev, tear down this wall" sort of way, but more like when you finally get the punchline to a joke everyone's been telling for years. It's the proverbial "aha!" moment that makes you wonder how you missed it for so long.

The interesting, and quite honestly, a little weird, thing is that Ms. Cannon's clients kept reporting the same phenomenon during their hypnotic sessions—they'd encounter the same souls over and over across different lifetimes, just wearing different costumes in the sitcom of existence. Can you imagine your annoying boss in this life might have been your best friend in 1847? Or your mother-in-law who drives you up the freaking wall could actually be your spiritual study buddy who agreed to push all your emotional hot buttons to help you grow? Let that sink in for a minute ... pretty wild, huh? I know, believe me, I get it. It sounds like something you'd come up with after too many glasses of bourbon and a paranormal documentary binge on Netflix. But stick with me here.

The thing is, once you start seeing people as part of your spiritual curriculum, rather than random obstacles in your day, everything shifts. Think of it this way: That person who cut you off in traffic isn't just an asshole—they're potentially a soul you've known for centuries, giving you another chance to practice patience. Or they could just be an asshole. The jury's still out on that one. (But even assholes are part of the unity consciousness, so there's that.)

What Ms. Cannon noticed was that people in this stage stop seeing separation as real and start recognizing everyone as extensions of the same universal consciousness. It's like realizing you've been arguing with different parts of yourself in the mirror your whole life. Talk about a cosmic plot twist. The practical result? You actually start giving a shit about other people's well-being—not because you should, not because it's the "spiritual" thing to do, but because you finally get that their success is your success, their pain is your pain, and we're all just trying to figure out this whole existence thing together.

So, does it make sense to you now? Do you understand why I have these two songs ping-ponging around in my head like some kind of spiritual earworm convention? We *are* the world in which we live, and we *are* all connected. Instead of the us-versus-them mentality that many of us have been preprogrammed with (thanks, society), we need to insert the magic word: love. Hence, "One Love." One heart. One existence and one big connection with each other. This is where my friend Dr. Julie Foster's expertise comes crashing in like a beautiful battering ram of consciousness. If you remember, Julie authored the book *Remembering Awake: How to Love and Play Creation with Y/our Soul.* I decided that I would go straight to the horse's mouth, or in this case, the incredible mind and spirit of Dr. Julie Foster, MD, to have her explain this section with me. Who better, right?

Dr. Foster discussed her God particle theory with me to help me truly understand it. Every stage of the awakening is beautiful and vital, but this stage seems to bring things all together. I guess a pun was intended there; no apologies for that. Unity consciousness may be something you have to work on initially, but it quickly becomes a situation where empathy stops being something you have to work at and starts being something you can't turn off—like a spiritual faucet that won't stop running, except instead of water, it's compassion, and instead of calling a plumber, you just learn to swim in it. I have had the good fortune of calling Dr. Julie Foster a friend for the past two years, and I can say that it has been life-changing, to put it mildly. Julie's gifts and her perspective have helped me understand some of the feelings and emotions I have been unable to articulate to this point. Have you ever had a conversation with someone and you ask, "Does that make sense?" after attempting to explain something to them? Well, that happens a lot when I speak with Julie, and of course, it makes sense to her. Julie is the embodiment of a star going supernova—brilliant, expansive, and illuminating everything in her vicinity.

What I'm about to say isn't sacrilegious in any way; the Bible actually refers to this statement in Genesis (not the *Abacab* album, by the way—that's Phil Collins, different kind of Genesis). I admittedly am no Bible scholar, so I had to do what any of you might have to do, and I GTS'd it. In Genesis 1:26–27, the Bible indicates that humans are created in the divine likeness and with the essence of God. God created humanity "in our image, in our likeness," and gives humanity a soul through God's breath (Genesis 2:7). This image or likeness of God, *imago dei,* is a reflection of God's nature, free will, a moral compass, and social interactions, which separates us from God's other creations.

Now hold on to your hats as I go down this rabbit hole with you all. So...if there's a part of God in each and every one of us, then we are all connected to God through his creation of man. It stands to reason, then, that we are all connected by that piece, or as Julie refers to it, the God particle that each of us has. So, if we all have the God particle inside of us, then we all have a common link or bond to one another. And if we are all connected, there is no separation or anything that is keeping us from being connected, which ultimately means that separation is an illusion.

Mind. Blown. Yet? We are all part of a humongous, interconnected whole, which allows us to share in each other's energies and experiences as a collective. This also explains why, when we are open, we can feel other people's energies, moods, frequencies, whatever you'd like to label them. It's not woowoo; it's physics meets metaphysics having a baby, and that baby is named Unity Consciousness. By not only understanding this principle but also living it, we are then able to have greater empathy, compassion, and understanding for those we meet. Everyone we meet is a part of our own spiritual journey. This further explains what I referenced previously in my meeting with Pat Longo, where it felt like we had known each other for my entire life. We likely had experienced several lifetimes together in some form or fashion, which is why we felt such a comfortable connection with each other. It wasn't just good vibes—it was soul recognition at its finest.

So what does all of this mean to us, to you, and to me? I think this means that there are no boundaries or limitations on us. We have nothing preventing us from having a deeper level of understanding and appreciation for one another, eliminating the need to separate ourselves from others, which allows us to be kinder and more understanding of the person you may have thought was different, or who you were frustrated with. We are one giant being, and when things come up that trigger emotions, it isn't that person; it's you who is working through something, and not the person who is the "cause" of your issue. We can choose to love ourselves in that moment of pain or frustration, because we aren't looking at someone else, really; we are only looking at another part of who *we* are.

It's like the universe is playing all the parts in a one-being show, and sometimes it forgets and starts arguing with itself. Road rage? You're yelling at yourself in another car. Office drama? You're gossiping about yourself. Family dysfunction at Thanksgiving? You're passing the mashed potatoes to yourself while judging yourself for taking a second helping. Once this really clicks—and I mean really clicks, not just intellectually but in your bones—everything changes. Kindness becomes natural because you're being kind to yourself, right? Forgiveness becomes easier because you're forgiving yourself. And love? Well, love becomes the only thing that makes sense or really matters. Because, at the end of the day, it's all "One Love" anyway.

Spiritual Summary

Unity consciousness is where the spiritual rubber meets the cosmic road. This stage isn't only about understanding that we're all connected—it's about living from *that* understanding every single day. It's recognizing that the homeless person in the alley, the CEO in the corner office, your annoying neighbor with the yappy dog, and your beautiful grandmother who adores you are all different faces of the same universal consciousness, each having a unique experience.

The God particle theory that Dr. Foster shares helps us understand that we're not just spiritually connected in some abstract way—we literally carry the same divine essence of God within us. Every person you meet is God in disguise, playing hide-and-seek with itself. Sometimes the disguise is really good (I'm looking at you, yes you, person who steals your coworkers' goodies from the office fridge), but it's still "the divine" having an experience.

This stage transforms everything: Relationships become opportunities for self-discovery, conflicts become chances to heal collective wounds, and service to others becomes service to the whole—including yourself. You stop asking, "Why is this happening to me?" and start asking, "What is this teaching me/us?" Because in unity consciousness, there is no "me" and "them"—there's only "us," and that we're all members of this cosmic orchestra playing our parts together.

Remember, unity consciousness isn't about losing yourself—it's about finding yourself in everything and everyone. It's the ultimate plot twist in your spiritual journey: You've been surrounded by yourself all along, just wearing billions of different costumes. And once you get the universal joke, you can't help but laugh at the incredible humor of it all.

Mastery and Service:
"Don't Stop Believin'"

I t's the final countdown, let the pigeons loose, cue the band! We made it, we're finally here, we did it, we've reached the final stage in the Spiritual Awakening Decathlon. The big kahuna. The spiritual black belt. The … okay, I'll stop with the overly dramatic buildup, but seriously, we've come a long way together, haven't we? From that first whisper of awakening, or in my case, some voice telling me, "*No*, this isn't your story, this isn't the end," to unity consciousness, and now here we stand at mastery and service. And what better anthem for this stage than Journey's "Don't Stop Believin'"?

"Don't Stop Believin'"
Journey

Because let me tell you something—after everything you've been through, all the dark nights of the soul, all the ego deaths, all the moments where you thought you were losing your mind (spoiler alert: You were just losing your old programming that no longer served you), you didn't stop believing. You couldn't. Something deeper than your conscious mind kept pulling you forward, cheering you on, and here you are.

But let's clear something up right away: Mastery doesn't mean you've got it all figured out. If someone tells you they've completely mastered spirituality, run. Run fast. Run like you're being chased by a horde of multilevel marketing representatives trying to sell you essential oils or an ancient Tibetan leaf from Buddha's Bodhi Tree that will "totally align your chakras." Take it from someone who bought that dried-up leaf. Because mastery, in Dolores Cannon's framework and in real life, isn't about perfection—it's about integrating what you've learned and experienced. It's about taking everything—the whole enchilada—that you've learned through these stages and living it. Every. Single. Day.

You know what mastery really looks like? Let me paint a realistic picture for you. It looks like me having a complete meltdown in Woodman's parking lot because they were out of my favorite black lager, then catching myself mid-tantrum and laughing because I recognize my ego is having a terrible-twos moment. It's knowing all about unity consciousness and still flipping off the guy who cut you off in the construction zone on 290 east—but then immediately sending him love because you recognize he's probably having a worse day than you. Or maybe he really needs to be 2.8 seconds ahead of you to save the life of a loved one in need. Who knows? The universe works in mysterious ways, and sometimes those ways involve letting jerks cut in front of you on the expressway.

I remember calling Kelly Schwegel one day, completely frustrated because I'd just had an argument with someone who pushed every button I thought I'd already healed. "Kelly," I said, "I thought I was past all of this petty shit. I thought I was more evolved than this, more enlightened." She laughed—that knowing laugh that spiritual teachers have when you're missing the obvious. "Jim, Jim, Jim," she said, "mastery isn't about not having any buttons. It's about knowing when they're being pushed and choosing how to respond to the bony finger pushing them. The fact that you're aware of it? That's real mastery in action." She was right. Again. I've found that she is annoyingly right a lot of the time.

Mastery is messy. It's human. It's divine. It's all of those things, all at once, all the time. It's knowing you're a beautiful soul or light body, having a human experience, and still capable of becoming unhinged when someone does something that disrupts your vibe (how human of you). It's understanding the illusion of time and still being perpetually five minutes late to everything. It's potentially all of those things, all wrapped up into what you lovingly call *you*. The beautiful paradox of mastery struck me during a coaching session I conducted last year. Here I was, supposedly a "master coach" (it says so on my certificate and everything, so it must be true), and in the middle of the session, I completely forgot what I was doing. Not like "forgot a word or a slide" forgot, but like "why am I here again, and what was I talking about, what the fuck is going on" forgot. For a split second, I panicked. Then I remembered: Mastery isn't about knowing everything; it's about trusting the process even when you might be a bit lost.

So I just stood there, blankly staring at the group of business leaders I was coaching, basically winging it while pretending I knew exactly what I was doing. And you know what? It turned out to be one of the most powerful coaching sessions I'd ever had. The group had a massive breakthrough, as if I had just shown them how to use a newfangled thing called a computer. When they asked me afterward where I found that information and how I knew that they had been looking for this kind of information for years, I wanted to say, "That was the old I-have-no-fucking-clue principle," but instead I just smiled mysteriously and said, "I followed what I was sensing was needed from all of you."

That's mastery—being comfortable with not knowing while appearing to know something. It's the spiritual equivalent of being a duck: calm on the surface, paddling like hell underneath, and occasionally quacking a profanity at inappropriate times. And here's the thing about the service aspect that Dolores Cannon understood extremely well: Service isn't something you do; service is something you become. It's not about signing up for every volunteer opportunity or becoming a spiritual martyr. God knows we have enough of those already, and they're exhausting to be around. "Oh, I couldn't possibly take a break. The universe needs me to hold space for everyone's trauma while neglecting my own needs." No, Karen, the universe needs you to take a shower and eat something besides raw almonds, rainbows, and good intentions.

Honest service, mastery-level service, is a different kind of service. It sneaks up on you. One day, you realize that you've been serving all along, just by being yourself. Every time you chose love over fear, every time you shared your weird spiritual experiences (even when people looked at you like you'd grown a second head), every time you simply held space for someone without trying to fix them—that was service.

Pat Longo exemplified this perfectly. When I met her, I expected some ethereal being floating three inches off the ground, speaking only in profound quotations. Instead, I got a down-to-earth woman who laughed at my jokes, complained about New York traffic, and occasionally dropped a swear word while channeling profound spiritual wisdom. She served not by being "spiritual" but by being real. And her authenticity gave everyone around her permission to be their authentic selves as well. She once told me, "Jim, the greatest service you can provide is to stop pretending you have it all figured out. People need to see the real you, the vulnerable, sensitive, authentic you. The 'you' that can still occasionally eat half a pizza and a six pack, while crying during *Field of Dreams*." (Okay, she didn't say exactly that, but it was something similar. I might have been embellishing about the pizza and beer thing.) The service component at this stage becomes as natural as breathing. You're not serving because you should, or because it's the "enlightened" thing to do. You're serving because you literally can't help it. It's like when you know a great restaurant—you just can't help but tell people about it. Except in this case, the restaurant is consciousness, and the special of the day is awakening with a side of existential crisis thrown in.

My service showed up in the weirdest ways. Sure, there were the obvious ones—coaching, writing this book, having deep spiritual conversations with anyone who would listen (and some who wouldn't—sorry to that guy at the gym who just wanted to use the elliptical machine in peace). The real service happened in unexpected moments. Like the time I was in line at Target (again with the lines—apparently, the universe thinks lines are spiritual training grounds), and I overheard a mom completely losing it on her screaming toddler. Instead of judging her or offering unsolicited parenting advice, I just sent her massive waves of love and understanding. I remembered my own meltdowns and moments of not being able to cope with my screaming, tantrum-throwing boys. The toddler stopped crying, and the mom's shoulders relaxed; she gave me a look—like she knew something had shifted but couldn't quite place what it was. That's service: anonymous, unglamorous, and one hundred percent essential.

Dr. Julie Foster once explained to me that mastery is really about becoming a conscious participant in creation rather than an unconscious victim of it. "When you reach mastery," she said, "you realize you're not just in the game, you are the game—you're simultaneously the player, the game piece, the board, and the dice. And once you know that, you can start playing with intention and love, rather than reaction." This blew my mind harder than the time I accidentally ate a whole mushroom brownie, thinking it was a regular brownie. (Pro tip: Always be sure to label your baked goods clearly when you bring that shit to a get-together.)

The thing is that mastery doesn't mean you stop having human experiences. You still get triggered. You still have bad days. You still occasionally tear up during commercials featuring dogs in cages that are mistreated. (Thanks, Jewel.) The difference is awareness and integration. You're having the experience while simultaneously observing yourself having the experience. It's like being the actor and the audience at the same time. Sometimes you're giving an Oscar-worthy performance of a "Human Having a Breakdown," and other times you're just phoning it in, and both are perfectly acceptable things.

I had a moment last month that perfectly embodied this. I was having a wonderful spiritual experience at the local park, feeling connected to everything, radiating positivity and light, like a freaking walking, talking Instagram inspirational quote. Then I got home, and my son's dog had eaten a book by an author who was going to be on my podcast. There was a notice about a bill I had forgotten to pay, and my neighbor was having what sounded like a quinceañera with a thousand guests. Within minutes, I went from being an enlightened being to raging against the machine, which was my life at that moment.

So here's the mastery part: I watched myself getting angry. I observed the rage rising, noticed my thoughts going to dark places (involving creative revenge scenarios with my neighbor's lawn ornaments), and then I just . . . laughed. Why did I laugh? I laughed because at that moment it was all so perfectly human. So beautifully ridiculous. Here I was, supposedly a highly evolved, spiritual being, plotting my revenge on my neighbor's cement flamingo and raincoat-wearing goose. That's when it hit me like a two-by-four across the head: Mastery isn't about transcending the human experience. It's about fully embracing it while remembering who you really are. It's about being able to hold both truths simultaneously—you are infinite consciousness and compassion, while also being someone who gets irrationally upset about books and mariachi bands.

The service aspect becomes even more interesting at this level. You realize that sometimes the greatest service you can provide is to simply be yourself, unapologetically and authentically yourself. Your "weird" becomes someone else's permission slip. Your struggles become someone else's roadmap. Your failures become someone else's hope that they, too, can crash and burn, while still being worthy of love and awakening.

Jen Weigel understood this when she encouraged me to share my story. "Jim," she said, "your journey isn't just yours. It belongs to everyone who needs to hear it. Your vulnerability is your superpower." At the time, I thought she was being metaphorical. Now I realize she was being literal. Every time I share my weird experiences, my doubts, my "did that really happen, or was it something I ate?" moments, someone says, "Oh, thank God, I thought I was the only one."

That's service. Not having all the answers, but being willing to share your questions. Not being perfect, but being perfectly willing to show up and share your imperfections. And here's something they don't tell you in a lot of spiritual books (well, except this one, apparently): Mastery can be hilarious. Once you really get the cosmic punchline—that we're all

God pretending to be separate, getting upset about things that don't really matter, taking everything so seriously when we're essentially in a giant cosmic sandbox—you can't help but laugh. I'm not talking about spiritual bypassing, where you laugh off real pain or dismiss genuine suffering, which is something I still do from time to time. I'm talking about the deep belly laugh that comes from recognizing the absurdity of the divine sitcom we're all starring in. Like the time I was in deep meditation, experiencing profound visions and feeling connected to all that is. Then I opened my eyes to find my neighbor staring at me with a quizzical look, which had me immediately question everything. Was I having a spiritual awakening, or was I just that weird guy sitting on a chair in the garage, with incense on his left and a cigar smoldering on the right? The answer we now know, of course, is both.

Kelly Schwegel summed it up perfectly during one of our sessions: "Jim, mastery is when you can hold the paradox without needing to resolve it. You can be enlightened and confused. You can be a teacher and a student. You can be awakened and still hit the snooze button five times every morning." And that's exactly what this stage is about. It's about integration, not perfection. It's about service, not sacrifice. It's about being divinely human and humanly divine. It's about knowing that you're exactly where you need to be, even when where you need to be is in your pajamas at 5 p.m., eating cereal for dinner, and wondering if your enlightenment can still be returned to Amazon.

The "Don't Stop Believin'" part? That's *huge*. Because mastery doesn't mean you've arrived at some final destination. It means you've realized the journey itself is the destination. Every day brings new opportunities to forget everything you know and remember it again. Every interaction is a chance to serve simply by being present. Every moment is both a test and a celebration. Some days you'll feel like a spiritual master, doling out wisdom and radiating light. Other days, you'll feel like you're back at square one, questioning everything and wondering if maybe you just made the whole thing up. Both are part of mastery. Both are perfect. The truth is, reaching this stage doesn't mean you have superpowers (although sometimes weird shit does happen—like knowing who's calling before you look at your phone, or finding parking spaces with suspicious regularity). It means you've learned to dance with the mystery, rather than trying to solve it. You've learned to surf the waves of consciousness instead of wiping out. You've learned that serving others and serving yourself are the same thing, just viewed from different angles.

Spiritual Summary

Mastery and service represent the integration of all the previous stages into a lived, embodied experience of awakened consciousness. This isn't your graduation or a finish line—it's more like getting your driver's license for consciousness. Now you know how to operate the vehicle, but the road trips are just beginning.

At this stage, you embody several key paradoxes without needing to resolve them:

- You are infinite consciousness, *and* you still get batshit crazy.
- You understand universal love, *and* you still have people who annoy the hell out of you.
- You know everything is perfect as it is, *and* you're still open to what the universe has in store for your highest good.
- You are the teacher *and* the eternal student.

Service at this level isn't about doing good deeds to earn spiritual merit badges. It's about recognizing that your very existence, when lived authentically, *is* service. Every time you choose love over fear, every time you share your truth, every time you simply show up as yourself, you're serving the collective awakening.

Mastery means you've internalized the lessons of each stage:

- **Awakening:** You remember there's so much more than meets the eye.
- **Questioning:** You remain curious and open to new ideas and thoughts.
- **Seeking:** You trust your inner guidance and where it leads you.

- **Finding:** You know where home really is, and you are always home.
- **Healing:** You've integrated your shadows and are healing them.
- **Purpose:** You know why you're here.
- **Service to Others:** You understand giving and receiving are one and the same.
- **Expanded Consciousness:** You can access different states at will.
- **Intuition:** You trust your inner knowing; you always know.
- **Manifestation:** You cocreate your reality consciously.
- **Unity Consciousness:** You see God and yourself in everyone.

All of this becomes not something you wear, but something you are.

Remember, you didn't come this far just to come this far. You came here to remember who you are, to integrate that remembering into every cell of your being, and to serve the awakening of consciousness simply by being yourself. That's mastery. That's service. That's the universe's joke that actually becomes a cosmic gift. And the journey? It never really ends. It just gets more interesting, more integrated, and more fun. Because once you know you're playing a game, you can finally start enjoying it. "Don't stop believin'," my fellow spiritual travelers. The best is yet to come. And the best part? You already are what you're seeking. You always have been. You just had to take the long way around to remember it. And what a beautiful, messy, perfect journey it's been.

"She Talks to Angels":
Communicating with Spirit

Since we've wrapped up all twelve stages of my personal account of having a spiritual awakening together, I thought you might want to know a little more about my experiences I had with some of the gifted individuals I had the pleasure of working with. "She Talks to Angels" by the Black Crowes is such a kick-ass song—it's even more awesome when you know a person who can actually communicate with angels.

"She Talks to Angels"
The Black Crowes

I'm not talking about someone who thinks their cat is giving them divine messages. (Though honestly, cats probably are interdimensional beings, so who knows?) I'm talking about someone who legitimately channels celestial beings. I've already mentioned this person earlier in the book, and that person is none other than Ms. Heather Sprigg. Heather is known as an angel intuitive, which in her case means she communicates with angels—specifically, she channels Archangel Michael, as well as Gabriel, Haniel, Ariel, Metatron, Azreal,

Raphael, Jesus, Mother Mary, a seraphim angel named Faith, Heather's higher self, oh, and God. And before you roll your eyes, thinking, "Oh great, another person who talks to angels after too much wine," let me tell you, Heather is the real deal. She's not wearing flowing robes and speaking in ethereal whispers. She's a down-to-earth person who just happens to have a direct line to the angelic realm. It's like having a friend who's really good at tech support, except the tech support is for your soul and the technician has wings.

Heather had been working on past-life regressions with her coach and mentor, Pat Longo (yes, the same Pat Longo who basically adopted me spiritually), and wanted to employ what she'd learned. She asked me if I'd be willing to have a session with her to see how it went. Who was I to say no to such an invitation? It's not every day someone offers to help you remember who you were before you were you. Plus, I was curious. Would I discover I was someone interesting? A pirate? A philosopher? A really successful peasant? The guy who invented bread? (Someone had to, right?)

What I'm going to do now is share a few excerpts from the transcript of my regression below. I have not gone through the transcript until now, so what you'll read is what happened that very day. I didn't have a transcription of the session until I found a software program to write everything out for us to read. I say "us" because I have not seen or read the transcript of my past-life regression until now. It's like opening a time capsule of my own consciousness. My hope is that this will give you a glimpse into what actually happened during my time with Heather.

Fair warning: What you're about to read might make you question everything you thought you knew about reality, reincarnation, and whether I'm completely full of shit, or not.

Spoiler alert: I'm not, but I wouldn't blame you for wondering anyway.

[Session Transcript Begins]

Heather: Let us go back to your childhood as you stay in the deeply relaxed, calm, and peaceful state. Let your deepest mind find a childhood memory. If you wish, you can keep it a pleasant memory, but you are free to choose. If at any time you become uncomfortable, just imagine yourself back in your peaceful garden, resting. You are always in control. If you wish, you can just float above the scene, watching it as if from a distance, or you can be in it, feeling it, seeing it vividly, colors in detail, and with emotions and feelings. This is up to you. Go back to your childhood, pick out a memory. It may be something you have not thought of or remembered for a very long time. Spend a few moments here, remembering vividly, seeing, feeling, using all of your senses. Do you have a memory?

Jim: Yes.

Heather: How old are you?

Jim: Two or three?

Heather: What do you see and what do you feel?

Jim: I'm in the backyard of my grandparents' house. And it's a spring day. There's a slight breeze, and we're playing with a paper kite, and Bucky, the dog, is there, and we're just running and laughing, and we're tying a tail on the kite so it can fly better.

Heather: How are you feeling as you do this?

> **Jim:** I'm very happy. I'm smiling, laughing, and running. I'm tripping in the grass and just laughing and getting up. I feel safe . . . Just happy.

Heather: So, you feel safe and happy in this memory.

> **Jim:** Yes.

Heather: Is that something that you don't feel now?

> **Jim:** Yes . . . I don't feel that way right now.

[End of First Excerpt]

Okay, so I can tell you this: I have not thought about a kite, let alone a paper kite, since my boys were toddlers and pre-K-aged children. I also hadn't heard the name Bucky in forever. At least not being used as a dog's name. I have, of course, heard the name Bucky used in the *Captain America* movies, but I'm pretty sure my grandparents' dog wasn't the Winter Soldier. Though he did have a habit of stealing food off my plate, so maybe there's a connection there. The thing that really got me was how vividly this memory came back. Not just the visual of it, but the feeling. That complete, uncomplicated happiness that only exists when you're three years old and the biggest concern in your life is whether the kite tail is long enough. No bills, no existential crises, no wondering if you're living your purpose. Just you, a kite, a dog named Bucky, and pure joy. Holy shit, right? But wait, it gets weirder. Let's move on to another section of the past-life regression. In this section, as you will see, we have a guest who decided to join in the fun. And by "guest," I mean my higher self chose to crash the party like an uninvited relative at Thanksgiving.

[Session Transcript Continues]

Heather: Do you have any thoughts or memories of why you are incarnating?

Jim: To make amends.

Heather: Do you know what you are here to make amends for?

Jim: For taking my own life.

Heather: Is there anything else you'd like to bring forward right now from this memory?

Jim: No matter the pain, I have to see it through.

Heather: Have you seen it through?

Jim: No, not yet … I'm not done.

Heather: Do you have anything you'd like to share with your current self that might help you along this process?

Jim: You're never alone. It's never as bad as you think. *[mumbled]*

Heather: What was that last thing?

Jim: It's never as bad as you think.

Heather: Is your current self heading in the right direction to make those amends?

Jim: At times, yes.

Heather: Just to verify, am I speaking to Jim's higher self?

Jim: Yes.

Heather: The amends that he needs to make. Are they to make amends to the people in his life currently?

Jim: To himself.

Heather: He didn't reach his goal in his last life?

Jim: No.

Heather: Roughly what age was he when he ended his life?

Jim: Twenty-four.

Heather: And you have a time period or year for me?

Jim: The 1930s . . . in 1932.

[End of Second Excerpt]

Okay, here's the thing . . . Believe me or don't believe me, I have *zero* recollection of this conversation, and I mean *zero*! I had no clue what was being said at this point, nor where I was, nothing. I know that may seem hard to believe—it is for me too! As I'm typing all of this out, I'm listening to the recording, and I have to say, I know that's my voice, so it's clearly me. However, I sound as though I'm either drunk, sick, or asleep. Or possibly all three, which would be quite an achievement. None of those three things is beneficial when it comes to having a conversation with someone, yet my answers are intelligible and direct. It's all very strange to hear. I don't remember this part of the conversation at all! I know I'm repeating myself here, but holy shit, it's quite a lot to take in. Apparently, my higher self decided to take the wheel while my conscious self took a nap. It's like finding out you sleepwalked to the kitchen, made a five-course meal, cleaned everything up, and have no memory of it. Except instead of cooking, I was having a heart-to-heart with my eternal soul about past-life trauma. You know, normal stuff for a Tuesday.

The idea that I took my own life in 1932 at age twenty-four hit me like a ton of metaphysical bricks. This time period was during the Great Depression. What the hell happened? Did I lose all of my family's money? Did I lose other people's money? Honestly, I don't know, but I do have my thoughts on it. I will definitely have to belly up to the bar for another round of the Past-Life Regression cocktail, and see what really happened. I feel it's something important to know, but for now that's what I have to go on. What about the message that I'm here to make amends—not to others, but to myself? That's the kind of thing that makes you stop and reconsider every decision you've ever made. Every time I've been too hard on myself, every moment of self-doubt, every instance of not believing I was enough, were all connected to this past-life guilt I'd been carrying around like invisible luggage.

Let's push on, because I do know that the next section is the cherry on top of my freak-flag sundae. And if you didn't have your mind blown before, this for sure will light the fuse for you. This next section I can recall, as Heather asked me to remember it—at least that's what she told me after the session had completed. By the way, if you thought the previous stuff was wild, buckle up, buttercup. We're about to go full *Indiana Jones* meets *The Da Vinci Code* meets that guy at the party who swears he was Cleopatra in a past life, except with actual evidence.

[Session Transcript—The Big One]

Heather: Imagine now that you are back in the garden, and in front of you is a large and beautiful mirror filled with light. As you look into this mirror, you see the reflections of many, many mirrors, and in each of these mirrors, you are in a different time, a different place. Perhaps a different space or dimension, perhaps another lifetime. Feel yourself being drawn into one of these mirrors. . . . *[continuing guidance]* . . . Five. Four. Three. Going into the mirror, being drawn in. Two, nearly there. One . . . be there. Take a moment—if you have a body—look down at your feet and see what you are wearing. You may have shoes, sandals, furs, skin, or perhaps nothing at all. Then look up your body. Look at your skin, your clothes, your hands, the size, color. Look at the area, the geography around you. Are there buildings? Are there people? Find yourself. Let a date come to mind. Where are you?

Jim: A desert town.

Heather: Where is the desert town?

Jim: There's sand . . . trees. People are standing around listening.

Heather: What are they listening to?

Jim: To me, talking.

Heather: Are you a speaker on a platform?

Jim: I'm standing on a rock.

Heather: Can you stop for a moment and explain to me how you are dressed?

Jim: I'm barefoot. No . . . wearing something that looks like sandals. I'm wearing some sort of fabric thing, a tunic, and it's very loose; it helps with the heat.

Heather: What about your skin? What color is your skin?

Jim: Dark brown.

Heather: Tell me about your hair.

Jim: Black, curly, long.

Heather: Do you have a time period or a date for me?

Jim: With Christ, with Jesus.

Heather: Are you traveling with Him?

Jim: No, ahead of Him.

Heather: What are you on the rock speaking about?

Jim: His glory, where He comes from . . . Son of God.

Heather: Are you a disciple of His?

Jim: Yes.

Heather: Do you have a name?

Jim: I don't . . . I don't under . . . Ishmo . . . Ishmon . . . Shimon. Yes, Shimon.

Heather: And how old are you?

Jim: Twenty-four . . . young man, but look older, weathered, not all weathered, because of the sun.

Heather: How are you feeling as you're standing on that rock speaking about Jesus?

> **Jim:** Fulfilled . . . proud, to speak His word.

Heather: How is the audience responding to you?

> **Jim:** Some are grabbing my leg, in glory, they're not trying to hurt me . . .

Heather: Trying to be a part of it?

> **Jim:** Some . . . yes, some. Some, no. Some of them are shaking their heads and leave. But that's okay.

Heather: It doesn't bother you.

> **Jim:** *[with a small laugh]* Oh no, they'll see.

Heather: Did you say, they'll see?

> **Jim:** Yes, I'm here to speak the truth, here, speaking the truth.

[Later in the session]

Heather: Looking at the people in the audience, the people around you, and the people who you are traveling with, do you recognize anybody who is in your current life now?

> **Jim:** I see my friend. Very proud, filled with . . . joy.

Heather: What is their relationship to you in the life you're in right now?

> **Jim:** My friend, a friend, dear friend. Yes.

Heather: Now I want you to move forward or backward a little bit, to when you are around Jesus. Are you there?

Jim: Yes.

Heather: Is this before or after you were speaking on the rock?

Jim: It's before.

Heather: What are you doing at this moment?

Jim: Sitting at His feet by a fire, it's a small fire, listening to Him. So good. So good. So much love. So good.

Heather: Please repeat that.

Jim: So much love.

[End of Main Transcript]

What did I tell you? Hey, if that didn't blow your mind, I don't know what would. The thing you should know about me for this to make more sense is that I am not a super religious person. Don't get me wrong, I believe in God, but I didn't study religion, nor did I attend church regularly growing up or even now. My biblical knowledge extends to knowing that Noah had an ark, Moses parted something, and Jesus turned water into wine (which, let's be honest, is the miracle we all wish we could perform at parties). To then be a person—scratch that—a disciple of Jesus and going out ahead of him to essentially be his warm-up act is, well, pretty freaking amazing. I mean, imagine my spiritual résumé: Experience: speaking on rocks about the Son of God, crowd work in ancient Judea, and sitting by fires listening to Jesus. Additional skills: extremely adaptable; can wear sandals in desert heat and maintain enthusiasm despite mixed audience reception.

Here's something else you should know; I didn't remember everything from the regression. As a matter of fact, I woke up at 2:13 a.m. the following morning with the question burning in my brain: "Who is Shimon or Ishmon?" Not exactly the kind of thought that usually wakes me at two. Usually it's more like "Did I leave the oven on?" or "What was that noise?" But no, my subconscious decided to play Biblical Jeopardy at two in the morning. I, of course, did what you all would expect me to do, and I went into my office and GTS'd it. A gentle reminder: GTS = Googled That Shit. Because when you wake up at 2:13 a.m. wondering if you were a biblical figure, Google is obviously the first place to turn. I'm sure that's exactly what the ancient prophets would have done if they'd had gig-speed Wi-Fi. I typed in "Who was Shimon or Ishmon in ancient Aramaic time?" Something that's also noteworthy here: I had no freaking idea this was "ancient Aramaic time." That was something that popped into my head and made its way to the keyboard. That's when I found out who he/I was—Simon, later renamed Peter (the Rock) by Jesus—and I learned that Jesus's disciples would travel to villages and cities before Jesus to essentially announce his upcoming arrival. I shit you not, I knew *none* of this! I mean *zero*! My biblical education did not include the logistics of Jesus's travel arrangements. I didn't realize there were advance teams. I thought Jesus just showed up in places and people were like, "Oh, hey, it's that Jesus guy who does all of the miracle things!"

Apparently, there was a whole system to what they were doing. The disciples would go ahead, prepare the grounds, and let people know what was coming. We were basically the ancient equivalent of a promotional street team, except instead of handing out flyers or putting coupons on your car windows, we were announcing the arrival of the Messiah: same energy, same excitement, just slightly different stakes. I immediately shared my findings with Heather, which is insane, but she is two hours behind us time-zone-wise, so it was two hours less crazy to text her then. There's something surreal about texting someone at 2 a.m., "Hey, so I just found out I was one of Jesus's advance men. How's your night going?" We had a phone conversation hours later to discuss my findings, at which time she shared some messages from Michael with me. And when I say Michael, I mean Archangel Michael, not Michael from accounting. Those messages I won't share with you all now, but I promise to spill the beans another time, another place. One thing I can share with you now is that Heather informed me of Archangel Michael's involvement in my past-life regression.

I asked Heather if Archangel Michael was responsible for my choosing the particular lifetime I chose, and she said yes. "Archangel Michael pulled you away from the lifetime you were going to choose for yourself and made sure you went to the lifetime with Jesus." The interesting thing with that was the fact that I felt as if I were redirected toward a different mirror than I wanted to go toward. In the Zoom video Heather shared with me, I physically leaned to the right, while sitting in my office chair, and I even made a slight turn to the right, which put me in the direct path of the small mirror with that lifetime. Crazy, right? The next logical question to ask Heather was why did he do it, what was so important about me seeing this lifetime when I did? "Archangel Michael said that it was important for you to view the lives he had you view, so you were able to see that even though you have some low points in one lifetime, it does not mean that your soul is destined to continue to experience negative life experiences. He said that he wanted you to see that you had the joy and beauty of walking with Jesus and being one of His disciples, which is clearly a positive or high point with your soul. He also wanted you to see that even if you decide to end your life, you are not doomed to an eternity of misery and damnation. Archangel Michael said it was important for you to witness those things in this lifetime to enable you to continue traveling upon your current path. He also wants you to know that you should begin to call on your angels more often; they are anxious to assist you." Call on my angels more often? Okay . . . WTF?! Try wrapping your head around that tidbit and not judge yourself for everything you do on a day-to-day basis that's less than godly.

The connection between Peter (Shimon) being twenty-four when he was speaking truth on that rock and me taking my own life at twenty-four by jumping from a building in my past life? Holy shit. Talk about cosmic irony. Same age, two completely different choices. One life: standing on a rock, spreading divine truth. Other life: jumping from a building in 1932. The universe really said, "Hold my beer, I'll show you what the full spectrum of possibilities looks like!" Just as during Peter's time, it seems there are greater things ahead in this life—things I'm meant to share with others. But here's what really scrambled my brain: Heather told me I'm going to write another book. Another book? Are you kidding me? I never thought *this* book was even possible! I'm still processing the fact that I wrote about sitting at Jesus's feet and telepathy with my mom, and now there's supposedly another one percolating in my noggin. Wow, I'm sure Archangel Michael wouldn't steer Heather wrong (that's not really his style), so who knows? Maybe there's a sequel brewing in this old brain. *Did I Just Have Another Spiritual Awakening, or Was It the Menudo This Time?* The universe really loves keeping us on our toes, doesn't it?

Spiritual Summary

This past-life regression revealed layers of my soul's journey that I couldn't have imagined. The childhood memory of pure, uncomplicated joy with my grandfather and Bucky the dog showed me what it feels like to be truly safe and happy—something my adult self had forgotten was even possible. It was a reminder that this feeling isn't lost; it's just buried under layers of adult responsibilities and fears.

The revelation about taking my own life at twenty-four in 1932 explained so much about the underlying current of sadness and guilt I've carried in this lifetime. The idea that I'm here to make amends—not to others but to myself—completely reframed my understanding of self-compassion and why it's been such a struggle. Every moment of being hard on myself was potentially connected to this past-life wound that needed healing.

But the past life as Simon/Peter, a disciple of Jesus? That was the universe showing me the full spectrum of possibilities. In one life, I gave up at twenty-four. In another, at the same age, I was standing on rocks, speaking truth, feeling fulfilled and proud, serving something greater than myself. The message couldn't be clearer: We always have a choice between despair and purpose, between giving up and speaking our truth.

The recognition of Heather as a "dear friend" from that lifetime explains the immediate connection and trust I felt with her. Soul contracts and soul families aren't just new age concepts—they're real, tangible connections that transcend space and time.

"Closing Time":
"Every New Beginning Comes from Some Other Beginning's End"

Well, we've covered a lot of ground, you and I. We've really gone through some heavy shit; I'm talking about *huge*, life-changing events. The kind of stuff that makes you question reality, sanity, and whether or not you should have eaten that gas station sushi that one time. (The answer is *no*, by the way. The answer is always *no* to gas station sushi. That's not spiritual wisdom; that's just good gastrointestinal advice.) I've shared some experiences with you that very few are privy to. Hell, there are things in this book I haven't even told some of my closest friends. Not because I don't trust them, but because how do you casually bring up over coffee, "Oh, by the way, I was apparently one of Jesus's disciples in a past life, and also I can carry on conversations with my dead grandpa now"? That's not exactly water cooler conversation. That's more like a "Holy Shit! Slowly back away from Jim" conversation.

I felt it was important to share it all with you. The beautiful, the ugly, the transcendent, and the absolutely batshit crazy stuff. Because I'm confident I'm not the only one in the world who has experienced something like this. Somewhere out there, someone is reading this while nodding their head, thinking, "Thank *God*, I thought I was the only one who cried during meditation and saw colors around people and wondered if I ate something funny, or I was having a spiritual awakening or a nervous breakdown." You're not alone. You're never alone. And I don't mean that in a creepy "someone's watching you" way. I mean it in the "we're all connected in this cosmic sitcom of consciousness" way. Which, okay, might still sound a little creepy, but you know what I mean.

Think about it for a moment—we went through the twelve stages of spiritual awakening together. From that first "What the hell is happening to me?" moment to the final "Oh, so this is what mastery looks like." (Spoiler alert: It looks a lot like normal life but with more awareness.) We walked through some of my experiences together, too. The good, the bad, and the "did that really just happen or did someone slip something in my drink?" We laughed together. (I hope.) We might have cried together. (I definitely did while writing some of this.) We probably both questioned my sanity at various points. (Join the club—I'm member number 001.) We've been through the stories of dead moms and glowing great-grandparents, of Disney World mayhem, and of total exhaustion and loss of hope that led to beach epiphanies. We've talked about signs from the universe that were about as subtle as a brick to the face, and others that were so gentle you might have missed them if you weren't paying attention.

Sure, we may have picked up some bumps and bruises along the way. Ego deaths aren't exactly known to be gentle. Healing childhood trauma isn't a walk in the park—it's more like a trek through an emotional jungle with no map, wearing flip-flops and a Speedo, while it's raining. And don't get me started on the losses. Losing my mom, losing my old sense of self, losing my ability to watch the news without feeling everyone's pain—these weren't easy. But let's not forget that those losses cleared the way for some profound discoveries.

Every ending made space for a new beginning. Every death (ego or otherwise) made room for rebirth. Every moment of "I can't do this" was followed, eventually, by "Holy shit, I did that." And that's my hope for you.

My wish for you is that you follow your heart and soul to allow yourself to become the bright shining light that you are. Yes, I know that sounds like something you'd find on an inspirational poster featuring a sunrise, probably in some funky font. But it's true. You are a light. Maybe you're more of a flickering candle right now than a blazing sun, and that's okay. Maybe some days you feel more like a burned-out light bulb that someone forgot to change. That's okay too. The light is still there, even when it doesn't feel like it. I hope this book gives you permission to be weird. To question everything. To trust your intuition even when it makes no logical sense. To cry in line at Disney World, if you need to. To laugh at the absurdity of this spiritual journey we're all on. To recognize that awakening isn't about becoming perfect—it's about becoming perfectly okay with being imperfect. Which is perfect.

I hope you find your Kelly Schwegel—that person who opens the door for your metaphysical curiosities. Your Pat Longo—who sees and feels your gifts, even if you don't, and then helps you to find and understand those gifts. Your Jen Weigel—who shows you that being spiritual doesn't mean you can't drop F-bombs, and who encourages you in all aspects of your life and pushes you to share your story even when it feels too vulnerable. Your Heather Sprigg—who talks to angels and helps you remember who you've always been. Your Dr. Julie Foster—who explains things that appear to be impossible to understand in ways that make sense. And last, but certainly not least, your Gail Alexander—who takes the time to explain and share her knowledge with you, to help you nurture and grow your gifts.

But most importantly, I hope you find yourself—the real you. Not the you that you think you should be, or the you that others expect you to be, but the you that *you* truly are. The divine wackadoo. The cosmic comedian. The spiritual warrior who sometimes battles anxiety with too much Mexican food and cervezas. The awakened being who still occasionally loses their shit in traffic, when some dumbass cuts you off. (Oops, namaste, man, namaste.)

No, my friend, this is not the end. How could it be? We're talking about spiritual awakening here, not a Netflix series. (Though honestly, someone should make this into a series, starring yours truly—call me, Netflix.) As the song says, "Every new beginning comes from some other beginning's end." Thank you, Semisonic, for that profound truth from Seneca disguised as a '90s closing-time anthem.

"Closing Time"
Semisonic

This book might be ending, but your journey? Oh, my friend, you're just getting started. You thought this was wild? Wait until you see what the universe has planned for act two. Or three. Or wherever you are in your spiritual screenplay. Remember: Every synchronicity is a wink from the universe. Every challenge is an opportunity for growth (annoying as hell, but true). Every person you meet might be a soul contract playing out, just for you. You may be asking yourself, What's this "soul contract" thing Jim's speaking of? Well, soul contracts are basically the universe's way of saying we signed up for this shit before we were born. Every difficult person we meet, every challenge, every "why me?" moment is apparently a lesson we preordered like cosmic DoorDash for our spiritual growth. You allegedly chose them backstage before this life-time to teach you patience, compassion, or how not to commit homicide. Once you realize you cowrote this screenplay, you stop being the victim and start seeing everyone as perfectly cast actors in your spiritual education—even if they're really committed to their role as "person who drives you up a wall."

Every moment is a chance to choose love over fear. And every day is an opportunity to remember who you really are—infinite consciousness having a human experience, probably while wearing a Led Zeppelin concert tee and wondering where you parked the car.

So, here's to you, fellow traveler. Raise your tequila, bour-bon, or beer high. Here's to your awakening, whatever that looks like. Here's to your journey, however it unfolds. Here's to the signs you'll see, the synchronicities you'll experience, the angels you'll meet (both the celestial kind and the ones who come in human suits). Here's to the breakdowns that become breakthroughs. Here's to the moments when you'll question everything and the moments when you'll know everything. Here's to finding your tribe of beautiful wingnuts who get it, who get you, and welcome you with open arms.

Thank you for sharing this adventure with me. Thank you for not judging me too harshly for the experiences I've shared. Thank you for sticking with me through the weird parts, the woo-woo parts, and the "wait, what the fuck did he say?" parts. Thank you for being open to the possibility that maybe, just maybe, there's more to this existence than what meets the eye.

And remember, if you ever find yourself standing on a beach at sunrise, feeling the pull of something greater, wondering if you're having a spiritual awakening or if it was something you ate—it's probably both. It's always both. That's the beautiful paradox of this journey.

"Happy Trails to You
Until we meet again.
Happy Trails to you
Keep Smilin' until then"
—Roy Rogers and Dale Evans

"Happy Trails"

Roy Rogers and Dale Evans

Peace out, and Happy Trails!

Later—

J

PS: If we do meet again, in this life or another, I'll be the one standing on a rock somewhere, probably talking too much about consciousness while wearing a tunic. Or . . . maybe I'll be the one sitting on the beach having a conversation with his departed great-grandpa, who decided to show up again after all these years. Either way, you'll know it's me. Just look for the person who seems to be having a spiritual experience and a human moment at the same time. Why choose between two good things? That's kind of how I roll now.

PPS: Don't forget to keep an eye out for the signs. They're everywhere. The universe is constantly trying to get your attention. Sometimes it whispers, sometimes it shouts, and sometimes it hits you with a cosmic two-by-four, like it did to me. Pay attention to all of it. Even the weird stuff. *Especially* the weird stuff.

PPPS: Yeah, yeah, I know that's too many postscripts, but this is my book and I'll PS all over the place, if I want to. Spiritual awakening doesn't mean you have to follow all the rules. Make your own rules. Dance to your own mystical music, like no one is watching. Write your own story. After all, you are the writer, producer, and director of this screenplay. And if that story includes excessive postscripts, F-bombs, synchronicities that blow your mind, and the occasional conversation with your higher self, well then, welcome to the club, our club.

Oh yeah, we meet on Tuesdays. Don't forget to bring snacks; we love snacks, man.

Thank you for reading the book!

Seriously—the fact that you made it to this page means something. If this book resonated with you, if it made you laugh or cry or question everything you thought you knew, then it did exactly what it was supposed to do.

I've created something special from me to you as a thank-you gift for purchasing and reading or listening to the book. When you scan the QR code below, you'll get access to everything that wouldn't fit between these pages: the spiritual summaries and reflection questions from each chapter (designed to help you go deeper into your own experiences), guided meditations, sound journeys, soundscapes, the full Spotify playlists that is the soundtrack for the book, and even the song I wrote specifically for our journey together. Hey, I've even included some cool things you may want to pick up for yourself or someone else, if Spirit moves you. Get it, if Spirit moves you?

This is exclusive content and the only way to access it is through this QR code. Consider it my way of saying thank you for trusting me with your time, your attention, and maybe allowing me to be a piece of your story.

Scan the code, and let's keep going!

https://qrco.de/bge5Az
Password: AteSomething@1

Acknowledgments

No journey like this happens alone or without a helping hand. I am deeply grateful to the people who walked with me, believed in me, and motivated me to keep going.

To **Nate Scripture** for your kindness, words of encouragement, your incredible sense of humor, and for being the undisputed Gif King.

To **Gail Alexander**, the Spiritual Swiss Army Knife, who is there to support me whenever I need it, and even when I don't.

Julie Foster, the tsunami of loving energy, who is always there for me to bounce crazy-ass ideas off.

Heather Sprigg, my angel sister, who never lost faith in me.

And **Jen Weigel**, holy cow, I don't have enough room to write everything you've done for me or mean to me. I have so much love and gratitude for you, and I'm thankful and proud to be called your friend.

To **Kelly Schwegel**, who knew that you were the teacher, mentor, and girl, I had been waiting for all my life.

You are the one who started me down this path, and I most certainly would not be here or have done this if you hadn't come into my life.

Pat Longo, the most loving, kind, and authentic soul I have had the good fortune to have met. I hope I made you proud with the writing of this book. And . . . I'm sure we did run in the same crowds in other lifetimes. You had such a profound impact on my life in such a short amount of time. Thank you for your words and your winks. Love and hugs to you.

And to **Kerry Sue Müller,** simply the best friend a person could ask for. You and your amazing husband, Camden, have welcomed me in and made me feel like family, and I love you both. Thank you for everything you've done to make this book a reality, P.P. I will never be able to thank you enough.

I love you all!

Peace—

J

About the Author

Jim Alstott spent most of his adult life as a practical, skeptical professional running an executive search firm, the kind of guy who believed in hard work, good data, and keeping both feet planted firmly on the ground. Then the universe had other plans.

What started as curiosity turned into a full-blown spiritual awakening that took him through past-life regression, energy healing, encounters with mediums, and experiences he still can't fully explain. Rather than keeping it to himself (or pretending it didn't happen), he did what any reasonable person would do: He started a podcast about it.

As host of *The Drop the Needle Podcast*, Jim interviews spiritual practitioners, mediums, energy healers, and consciousness researchers, always with genuine curiosity and a healthy dose of skepti— Wait, seriously . . . skepticism? The dude's a certified Reiki Master and Chios practitioner. Although he'll be the first to admit that he's still figuring out what that means.

Did I Just Have a Spiritual Awakening, or Was it Something I Ate? is his first book. He wrote it for everyone who's ever felt pulled toward something bigger but didn't want to lose their sense of humor or their bullshit detector along the way.

He lives in the Chicagoland area with his wife and three sons, still runs his executive search and coaching businesses, and continues to ask questions he doesn't have answers to.

Learn more at www.jimalstott.com or find him on *The Drop the Needle Podcast* at www.dtnpodcast.com or wherever you listen to podcasts.

www.ingramcontent.com/pod-product-compliance
Lightning Source LLC
Chambersburg PA
CBHW030917060726
47591CB00005B/1581